THE
PIG
THAT
FLEW

**THE BATTLE
TO PRIVATIZE
CANADIAN
NATIONAL**

THE
PIG
THAT
FLEW

HARRY BRUCE

Douglas & McIntyre
Vancouver/Toronto

Douglas & McIntyre
1615 Venables Street
Vancouver, British Columbia
V5L 2H1

CANADIAN CATALOGUING IN PUBLICATION DATA

Bruce, Harry, 1934–
  The pig that flew

ISBN 1-55054-609-0

  1. Canadian National Railways. 2. Railroads and state—
Canada. 3. Privatization—Canada. I. Title
HE2810.C14B78 1997   385'.06'571   C97-910651-6

Editing by Nancy Pollak
Cover photograph courtesy of CN
Cover design by Peter Cocking
Uncredited photos courtesy of CN
Text design and typesetting by Val Speidel
Printed and bound in Canada by Friesens
Printed on acid-free paper

The publisher gratefully acknowledges the support of the Canada Council for the Arts and of the British Columbia Ministry of Tourism, Small Business and Culture.

Excerpts from the following are reprinted with permission: *Double Vision: The Inside Story of the Liberals in Power* by Edward Greenspon and Anthony Wilson-Smith. Copyright © 1996 by Edward Greenspon and Anthony Wilson-Smith. Reprinted with permission of Doubleday Canada Limited.

Contents

Introduction

Before the privatization of Canadian National in the fall of 1995, business journalists viewed the railway as an investment disaster waiting to happen. They called it "clunky, clanky CN," "the creaky giant," "a lumbering overregulated bureaucratic giant," "a crown-owned basket case," "a state-owned monster," and not the national dream but "the national nightmare." It was "fat," "bloated," "inefficient" and "debt-ridden." Indeed, it was "a money-losing leviathan of metal and muscle," "a subsidy-consuming behemoth," "a dinosaur" and "the tyrannosaurus known as CN Rail."

CN shares would be "a dog stock" and the railway itself was "a dog on steroids." It was "a white elephant." It was "a pig." Worse, it was "a pig with lipstick." It had received "boxcars of subsidies," yet its debt was "off the Richter scale." CN was "the sad-sack national rail outfit that has had more fresh starts than Elizabeth Taylor has had husbands."

When Canadian business reporters exhausted their ability to dream up contrived insults for the railway, they extracted from investment bankers skeptical statements about the Initial Public Offering (IPO) of CN shares. To take one example, Fred Simons of Interinvest Consulting Corp., Montreal, declared that since a government mentality had long infected CN, "I have a hard time believing this is the Second Coming . . . Why should I trust a government-backed agency when I don't even trust the government to deliver mail?"

Disappointing privatizations in the United Kingdom and the botched sales of hunks of Air Canada and Petro-Canada further poisoned the atmosphere surrounding the CN deal. About certain underwriters, Toronto stockbroker Murray Pollitt said, "They all got skinned alive on Air Canada." As Wilfred Gobert, an analyst with Peters & Co., Calgary, put it, "When you take a hit, it makes you leery about sticking your neck out again."

Even members of the federal cabinet and senior bureaucracy saw CN as a loser, and the IPO as a looming failure. "There was a lot of skepticism in Ottawa," recalls Gerald K. Davies, CN's senior vice-president, marketing. "By and large, the Canadian government thought, 'Aw, you know, we'll never get this thing done.' "

It often seemed as though the only people who thought CN would be a good investment were Americans.

If the privatization of CN looked unpromising to Canadian business journalists, brokers and bureaucrats, it looked improbable to political junkies. "CN put up for sale by the Liberals?" the *Globe and Mail* marvelled. "If such a thing had occurred a few years ago, every economic nationalist in the land would have lashed himself to the tracks, singing Gordon Lightfoot and crying betrayal."

Weren't the Liberals the enemies of privatization? Wasn't it the Progressive Conservatives who had sold off pieces of Air Canada and Petro-Canada? "Since 1984, the government has privatized or dissolved thirty-nine crown enterprises and other holdings," Tory finance minister Don Mazankowski bragged in April 1993. "The number of full-time crown corporation employees has been reduced by nearly 90,000." The Tories were therefore the proven champions of privatization, and the Liberals had long felt it their duty to lambaste them for being so.

In August 1988, Jean Chrétien's predecessor as Liberal leader, John Turner, furiously accused the Tory government of selling some of Canada's most important institutions. His voice dripping with sarcasm, he asked, "Is Canadian National next?" On October 20, 1993, just five days before the Liberals returned to power, Chrétien wrote, "Their [the Conservatives'] continued tolerance of rail line abandonments and consideration of proposals for the privatization of CN Rail have done nothing to improve the situation. It will be up to a Liberal government to clean up this mess."

During the campaign that ended with the Liberals' victory on October 25, they hadn't promised the privatization of anything, much less that of the biggest and oldest of all crown corporations. Only sixteen months later, however, on February 27, 1995, finance minister Paul Martin Jr. uttered a sentence as astonishing as it was historic: "Today, we are announcing that the Minister of Transport will initiate steps this year to sell CN." Liberals still saw "privatization" as so detestably Tory they refused to use the word. They talked instead about the "commercialization" of CN. The privatization legislation, which transport minister Doug Young introduced in the House of Commons on May 5, 1995, was the CN Commercialization Act.

The year would see not only CN's privatization, but also the abolition of century-old federal subsidies for the shipping of Prairie grain by rail and the introduction of an act making it easier for CN and Canadian Pacific to sell or abandon unprofitable lines. The three pieces of legislation, *Railway Gazette International* explained, amounted to nothing less than "the most radical changes to the industry since the creation of Canadian National in 1923."

"No other public institution, apart from the Post Office, is as ubiquitous a presence [as CN] in so many Canadian communities," political scientist Garth Stevenson wrote. "Described in the novels of Hugh MacLennan, painted by the Group of Seven, and commemorated in song by Gordon Lightfoot, [the railways] remain deeply embedded in the national consciousness."

Millions of Canadians can still remember drifting off to sleep as children while the sad, urgent, faraway whistle of a Canadian National Railways train floated into their bedrooms. CNR sent "schools on wheels," as well as medical and dental clinics, into the remotest boondocks of Canada, erected landmark hotels all across the country, and pioneered telecommunications. CNR was once Canada's biggest employer; by 1955 it had 116,853 people on its payroll. It maintained no fewer than 5,000 stations. In hundreds of towns the CNR station was the major social centre. Engineers and conductors enjoyed almost as much social status as town doctors and mayors.

CNR was as Canadian as pucks, canoes, Mounties, beavers, grain elevators and the Canadian Broadcasting Corporation. Indeed, the railway had given birth to the CBC and Air Canada. Widely known in recent decades as CN, the line was once "The People's Railway," but now it would become simply a shareholders' railway. Discussing the privatization on CBC Radio's *Morningside*, one commentator complained, "It's our national dream on the auction block." He feared Americans would take control of Canada's beloved CN.

As though the investment climate weren't dismal enough for the CN IPO, the railway's top executives would undertake their supreme selling effort before, during and after the Quebec referendum on October 30, 1995. During twenty-one of the most gruelling yet exhilarating days of their lives, they would visit twenty-six cities in nine countries to pitch CN to hundreds of hard-headed and sometimes fiercely interrogative investment professionals. The CN men would be in Zurich when Canadian television tallied up the results of the referendum. The next day they would fly by private jet to Frankfurt and Rotterdam, and then drive on to Amsterdam.

But if Quebec voted to quit Canada, what would happen to the value of Canada's only coast-to-coast railway? What about its headquarters in Montreal and its other assets in Quebec? Who would invest in the national railway of a nation falling apart? When a reporter asked Toronto investment banker Gordon S. Lackenbauer what would happen to the IPO if Quebec's separatists won the referendum, he replied, "You don't have to be a rocket scientist to figure that you don't try to push product in that environment." As deputy chairman of Nesbitt Burns, he himself was one of the major pushers of the CN product.

So what did happen?

The separatists lost the referendum by a margin as thin as tissue paper.

Seventeen days later, the sale of CN shares made fools out of all those Canadians who had been dumping on it for months.

The shares were at least eight times oversubscribed. The demand was so powerful that, during an eleventh-hour meeting before the stock went on sale, men from the one American and two Canadian investment-banking houses that served as the deal's global coordinators engaged in a table-thumping squabble over the international division of the 83,800,000 shares in the IPO. A veteran underwriter from Toronto remembered the meeting, at the Montreal Airport Hilton, as the toughest and angriest he had attended in his entire life.

At stake, for each side, were millions of dollars in commissions. "In a situation like that," says Michael Sabia, a senior vice-president at CN and its chief financial officer, "greed is not a bad word. It's what makes things go."

Things certainly did go.

On the night of November 16, 1995, the government sold CN to the underwriters for $2.2 billion, making the deal the biggest IPO in

Canadian history. According to some, it was the biggest *transaction* of any kind in Canadian history. And when the New York, Toronto and Montreal stock exchanges opened on the morning of November 17, the share price rose at a speed that surprised even the most optimistic of the IPO's promoters.

This was not only the biggest IPO in Canadian history but the quickest. By Ottawa's standards, the speed of the campaign to privatize CN was nothing short of phenomenal. Between Martin's announcement that Young would take steps to sell CN, and June 20, when the House of Commons passed the necessary legislation, not four months passed. Between June 20 and the sale of CN, not five months passed.

Finally, the sale of CN not only broke records for its size and speed, it turned out to be the most rewarding IPO for investors that the government ever pulled off. Across Canada, headlines told the story: "CN Rail issue burns up the tracks" . . . "CN shares make hot debut" . . . "CN shares steam ahead from outset" . . . "Orders flood in for CN stock" . . . "Investors rush to board CN express" . . . "On Day One, CN stock zooms" . . . "CN shares jump $4 in ultra-hot Toronto Stock Exchange debut" . . . "TSE chugs up on CN shares" . . . "CN rescues poor Bay Street" . . . "Madness at its best" . . . "Smashing success."

Within a year the share price would double.

Back on that first heady day of trading, business reporter Ann Gibbens told listeners of *Radio Noon* in Montreal, "God forbid that we should give praise here, but I do think much of it should go to the two top people at CN, Paul Tellier and Michael Sabia. Ironically, these two are former bureaucrats."

"If Ann is going to break all the rules of journalistic ethics by praising people," business columnist Jay Brian added, "then I am going to say this is another economic initiative of the Chrétien government that seems to have worked out very well, coming on the heels of Paul Martin budgets that also worked out very well. So they are looking good on economic management."

CN's privatization, columnist Barry Critchley wrote in the *Financial Post*, was "a seminal example of how to sell state-owned assets."

This book is about how that privatization came about. The story involves cabinet-level intrigue, crushing workloads for CN's brass, corporate blood-letting, the elimination of thousands of jobs and the imposition of drastic changes to the whole culture of the old railway. The tale is about the scuttling of outdated and extravagantly generous labour agreements, the eruption of yelling matches behind closed doors, the collapse of merger negotiations with Canadian Pacific Rail, and in New York, Toronto, Montreal and Ottawa, the conflict and the teamwork among people as shrewd as they were willful, as confident as they were ambitious.

In the end, however, it wasn't only plans, brains, bold decisions and fifteen-hour working days that led to the success of what one journalist called "The Mother of All Sales." Accidents, the onslaught of unexpected pressures, the deficit-slashing policies of the Canadian government, Canada's crucial need to prove it could actually privatize a crown corporation properly, the bullish investment climate of North America—all these contributed to what Sabia described as "the proper alignment of the stars for the privatization of CN." Even things that went wrong eventually helped the privatization go right.

"The Wrong Man" Takes Over

P aul M. Tellier, bureaucrat *par excellence* and railway ignoramus, was exactly the sort of man the government should not have named boss of Canadian National. That, at least, was the early opinion of many union leaders, CN executives and rail-industry experts. News of his appointment broke in June 1992, but a year before that—when the search began in earnest for a successor to Ronald E. Lawless, sixty-seven, president and chief executive officer—the government heard admonitions not to replace this venerable CN statesman with a railway neophyte. Promote someone from the ranks of CN's able executives, railway people urged. Lure the chief of some hot American railway to Canada. Just don't give the job to a chum of the Conservative government who doesn't know a newsprint car from a vacuum pneumatic unloading hopper.

Larry Olson of the United Transportation Union, whose membership included 7,000 CN employees, warned that any newcomer would face not just a formidable learning curve, but a struggle to gain the confidence of workers. "Getting fresh blood in," he grimly advised, "may lead to CN's last gasp."

Lawless wanted John Sturgess to succeed him, and so did certain labour leaders. Sturgess was CN's senior vice-president and chief operating officer, and according to one union man, "second only to God" at the corporation. But he was also a CN devil whom the unions knew. They preferred him to a devil they didn't know, and with good reason.

"Over the years, we've got things from Canadian National we never dreamed of getting," Edward G. Abbot, executive secretary of the Canadian Railway Labour Association, later stated. "It's unbelievable how inefficient and ineffective they are at the bargaining table. Collective bargaining [with CN] is like playing poker with someone else's chips. You're bound to win."

Tellier's appointment, effective October 1, 1992, alarmed not only the unions, but also senior railroad professionals. In their eyes, his having managed government departments was inadequate training for running a deeply troubled national railway with yearly revenues of $4 billion. Why had Prime Minister Brian Mulroney chosen a man without a shred of railway experience, or even corporate experience, over CN vice-presidents who had spent their lives in the rail industry?

"Large corporations should have CEOs that have fought for and won through learning experience the right to head them," Roger Robinson, a CN engineer in Hamilton, Ontario, publicly complained. "This is not the time . . . for political appointees with no corporate exposure."

Tellier had never been a backroom boy or bagman for the Tories. His sin was simply having served as Canada's top bureaucrat. As clerk of the privy council and secretary of the cabinet, he attended meetings of both the full cabinet and its more important committees. He was chief of the entire federal bureaucracy, deputy minister to the prime minister, and as one business reporter wrote, "the consummate Ottawa insider." Ever since 1985, his critics claimed, he had been in Brian Mulroney's pocket.

Some saw the appointment as a prime example of the government meddling that for seven decades had sabotaged the railway's effort to operate like a real business. Mulroney had already appointed, as CN's chairman, West Coast lawyer and Social Credit politician Brian Smith. With Tellier in the president's chair, the corporation's two most powerful jobs belonged to railway tyros.

The suggestion that Tellier's appointment might prove to be a step towards CN's privatization struck industry-watchers as ludicrous. Hadn't Lawless tried for years to make CN lean enough to sell? Hadn't the government, leery of the political fallout from lay-offs and line abandonments, repeatedly refused to go the whole hog towards privatization? And hadn't this so-called superbureaucrat been part of that very government?

Forgetting that Tellier in government had been more servant than master, a former CN executive told Canadian Press reporter Alex Binkley, "So now you have a guy who fought many of the rationalization plans [while he was] in government, and he's put in charge of the company, and *that's* supposed to promote privatization!"

Had the naming of a new CN president ever before aroused such dismal expectations? When Tellier began to work with CN vice-presidents, their ignorance of his record surprised him. "Some people told me later, 'You know, we expected a stuffed shirt from Foreign Affairs,' " Tellier recalls. "Well, I can be described as a great many things, but anybody who had done any homework about what I'd been doing for the previous twenty years could never have described me as a stuffed shirt from Foreign Affairs."

Born at Joliette, Quebec, in French-speaking farm country north-east of Montreal, Paul Tellier was the fifth of Maurice and Eva Tellier's six children. Maurice was a lawyer, a Union Nationale politician and the speaker of the National Assembly in Quebec

City. Paul grew up so rebellious that various Jesuit colleges expelled him. After he quit a boarding school that he detested—to become a skiing instructor—Maurice persuaded him to go back to day school. He later earned a law degree at the University of Ottawa and in 1966 graduated from Oxford University with a graduate degree in public administration. He taught law at the University of Montreal, but soon moved to Ottawa as executive assistant to energy minister Jean-Luc Pépin. He expected to stay in government about a year. A quarter-century would pass before his move to CN.

By then, he was fifty-three and known in Ottawa not only for having a chauffeur-driven Jeep Cherokee, rather than the standard deputy minister's limousine, but for being a chameleon so skilled he had served Liberals and Conservatives with equal success. He was Prime Minister Pierre Trudeau's principal adviser on national unity, and later deputy minister for energy minister Jean Chrétien. When the Tories won the 1984 federal election, an Ottawa insider remembered, "People thought Tellier would be blown away by Patricia Carney [the strong-willed Conservative who replaced Chrétien in the energy portfolio] and just wouldn't survive. Not only did he survive, he flourished. He was *the* success story from a deputy point of view."

Tellier's fitness program reveals the intensity and focus with which he tackles the challenges that come his way. He rises before dawn to jog or to ride his mountain bike. He swims, plays squash and tennis, and skis—downhill, cross-country and on water. To combat backsliding, he keeps a diary. "So I can tell you," he says, "that last month I exercised 29 days out of 30. I keep monthly accounts, and at the end of the year, I'll be able to say I did my exercising on, say, 325 days. You've got to do it wherever you are in the world. I am close to a fitness nut. If I don't do it for two days, I feel awful." With visitors to his office, he sips cranberry juice.

For more than twenty years, Tellier has worked at least six long days a week. In times of crisis he puts in seven, "but I try usually, under normal circumstances, to take Friday night off and to take Saturday off."

Every Sunday morning, he gets his exercise, eats his breakfast and starts his work. "But I do it in a family environment," he says, thinking of his wife Andrée and their adult daughter and son. "I'm not asking the kids to be quiet or anything like that. I don't closet myself. I just sit at the dining-room table, and I work. And I enjoy it . . . So, you know, I'm not doing it like a monk. Very often my wife will say on a Sunday evening, 'Aren't you going to stop?' and I say, 'Listen, I'm not working, I'm enjoying myself.' "

The enjoyment includes riding herd on CN management. "Tellier keeps track of his obligations and those of his senior executives through a colour-coded filing system and an at-a-glance scheduling and duty roster that is time managed on a daily, weekly, and yearly basis," the *Financial Post* reported. "He reviews everything in detail, at home each Sunday, 'at my own pace for anywhere from four to ten hours.' "

"Very often, this [review] triggers some questions in my mind," Tellier explains, "and I phone them [the executives] and talk to them, and basically I catch up with my paperwork, and when I arrive on Monday morning, I've got two or three briefcases to empty, but everything is tidy, everything is ready. As a result, I am pretty relaxed about the whole week."

Tellier insists he's not a workaholic. "I consider myself well-balanced," he argues. "I have time for my family, I have time for my friends, I have time for sports and to keep myself in good shape. I have time to watch a good hockey game. But if I go to a hockey game on Monday night, very likely I'll work longer hours the next Sunday. I have to catch up . . ."

Applied to the Tellier whom Ottawa knew but the rail industry did not, "hard-driving" was a serious understatement. He pushed himself—and his subordinates—hard. "As someone once said," he told a reporter, " 'Tellier, you're never going to have ulcers because you provoke them in others.' "

"I'm a very impatient individual," he has also allowed, turning what some regard as a defect into a virtue. "One could see this as a quality, I suppose, because it gives a sense of urgency. I've heard the English expression, 'He does not suffer fools gladly.' I'm quite comfortable living with this description." An employee he decides is a fool or malingerer may hear from him directly. He can be as blunt as a bulldozer.

"I've known Paul Tellier for twenty-five years, and he had a meteoric career in the public service," recalled Gordon Ritchie, a one-time senior bureaucrat. "So his bluntness hasn't been a fatal handicap. And for most of those twenty-five years, he was in a very sensitive public capacity, dealing with national unity issues, the Department of Indian Affairs and Northern Development, and energy."

Gordon Robertson, a Tellier predecessor as Canada's Number One civil servant, said the new president of CN was "very used to making hard decisions and carrying them out."

That's exactly what cleaning up CN would require: hard decisions by a boss as tough as saddle leather.

CHAPTER 2

Was the Next Stop Bankruptcy?

By late 1991, Canadian National's brass knew that, unless they could find a way to switch their railway to a new track, it would hurtle into a tunnel of bankruptcy and never come out. There would be no government bailout this time.

A creature of government, Canadian National Railways arose in 1917–23 from the amalgamation of five financially troubled lines. These had been both the beneficiaries of pork-barrelling and the victims of corruption, corporate back-stabbing, blatant patronage and pie-in-the-sky salesmanship. Leftovers from the ultimately disastrous railway-building mania that swept Canada before World War I, they bequeathed to the new crown corporation a track network so huge it would never make business sense.

Early and long, CN endured the curses that had afflicted its forebears: not only too much trackage, but too much debt; too much political interference; and too much venom from Canadian Pacific. For generations, CP and CN, each a gigantic empire, bitterly faced off against each other. One privately owned and one government-owned, they were the stars of twentieth-century Canada's most conspicuous business rivalry.

Successive governments piously insisted CN perform like a competitive private business and adhere to sound principles of commerce, yet forced it to run money-losing lines, maintain obsolete workshops, buy rolling stock in a certain cabinet minister's bailiwick, purchase rails in Cape Breton to support the island's perpetually sputtering economy, and indeed provide all manner of unprofitable services to fulfil social policies and curry favour with voters. When a government changed, so did CN's board. A gang of Tories or Grits, knowing little about operating a transcontinental railway, replaced an equally unqualified gang of Grits or Tories.

CN plunged into financial messes so severe that governments, by forgiving debt or changing it to equity, granted this transportation conglomerate fresh starts in 1937, 1952 and 1978. Over decades, CN cost taxpayers tens of billions of dollars, and in 1978, the government decided to plug the leak forever. In a conversion of $808 million of debt into common stock, this supposedly final recapitalization slashed CN's annual interest payments by $65 million, but also stipulated that the corporation become financially self-sufficient. From then on, CN was to raise its capital entirely on its own. It would have to generate capital from earnings, borrow it from money markets or get it by selling assets. Moreover, CN would pay the government a 20 per cent dividend on whatever profits it reaped.

CN now waltzed into its headiest period since World War II. "We have recorded profits during all but two of the eleven years [since the 1978 recapitalization]," President Ronald E. Lawless boasted in 1989. "And rather than being a drain on the treasury, we have contributed $237 million in dividends to our shareholder."

CN's success, however, had come at a high price. For a dozen years, the corporation had been shedding businesses and dumping armies of workers. The government's creation of VIA Rail Canada in 1977 enabled both CN and CP to escape their historic obligation to run money-gobbling passenger services. (As late as 1995, one survey revealed that many Canadians still didn't know CN had quit the passenger business.) The government in 1985 turned CN Marine, the corporation's interprovincial and international ferryboat service on the East Coast, into a separate crown corporation, Marine Atlantic. After CN Route, a trucking outfit, lost $47 million in 1986, CN sold it to private investors (who promptly drove it into bankruptcy).

Further dismantling of Canada's biggest transportation and communications empire would follow a buildup of debt that dwarfed profits. Responding to a resource boom, CN had reached deep into its pockets to expand rail capacity in western Canada. Then the recession of 1982 whacked it, shoving net income into the red.

To make matters worse, what CN delicately called "imposed public duties for which the company received no compensation" were a millstone no privately owned railway would ever have tolerated. Lines in the Maritimes, Newfoundland and parts of the West dropped hundreds of millions of dollars. In 1986, when CN's net income again plunged into the red, its long-term debt soared to $3.4 billion. More than half of this monstrous burden, CN Chairman J. Maurice LeClair claimed, was the result of those imposed public duties. During 1987, CN paid interest of more than $1 million a day.

If the debt crisis gave it no choice but to sell cherished assets, neither did Prime Minister Brian Mulroney's Conservative government. Liberals had created most of Canada's crown corporations, and many of the Tories who took power in 1984 swore government had no business operating agencies that competed with private industry. Historically, Conservatives had backed CP and abused CN. "The Mulroney government's insistence that CN dispose of its profitable nonrail activities was in sharp contrast to the views of previous governments," Garth Stevenson of Brock University wrote in 1988, "and suggested that Tory 'hostility' to CN was by no means extinct in the 1980s."

In 1988, CN sold its chain of nine hotels to Canadian Pacific Hotels Corporation for $265 million; its 50 per cent share in CNCP Telecommunications to CP Ltd. for $235 million; and its telephone companies in the Northwest Territories for $208 million and in Newfoundland for $174 million. These deals, which reaped $882 million, enabled CN in 1989 to lower its long-term debt to $1.9 billion and bring its debt-equity ratio down from an alarming 53 per cent in 1986 to a respectable 35.3 per cent. Annual interest payments dropped from $372 million in 1987 to $199 million in 1989.

That fall, however, another recession descended on Canada. It would impose grim figures on CN's balance sheet.

Before resigning from CN in 1986, Chairman and CEO J. Maurice LeClair pointed to "a growing consensus that it must be fit and healthy before it can be offered as a candidate for private-sector investment." No one knew better than his chief lieutenant, President Lawless, just how unfit for privatization CN was. A bulky six-footer with a big, square face, a crop of thick straight hair, bushy eyebrows and a gold locomotive glittering on his necktie, Lawless was every inch the CN man. He joined the corporation as a seventeen-year-old customs clerk in the days of steam locomotives, and when he retired in 1992, had half a century's service under his ample belt. The press called him "the tough-talking president of Canadian National Railways" and "Canada's leading railway man," but by 1990 union leaders saw him as "The Slasher." In five years, he had cut CN's work force from 51,000 to 38,000.

Throughout much of the 1980s, CN wilted and shrank as competition got hotter and hotter. Truckers benefited not only from low costs of both infrastructure and labour, but from the ability to deliver a variety of goods door-to-door and precisely on time. They now dominated the Canadian freight business. "There was a monopoly attitude in railroads," Lawless explained in 1991. "We had one railroad, and Canadian Pacific was across the street, and what was there to worry about? There was no real competition . . .

But there was. The competition was the trucks, and we've seen the railways' share of market erode from 70 per cent [in the postwar years] down to 30 per cent."

Trucking, however, wasn't the only competition. On October 14, 1980, the U.S. Congress enacted the Staggers Act. Overnight, it freed American railways from regulations that had strangled some lines in the 1970s and left others gasping for air. By making it easier for railroads to set their own rates, strike confidential deals with shippers, abandon or sell branch lines, and participate in mergers and buyouts, the legislation launched an American revolution in transportation efficiency.

Competitive forces now lunged at the U.S. rail industry, chopping off its flab. By 1985, the number of Class 1 railroads had dropped from forty-one to twenty-two, and their total work force had plummeted from half a million to just over 300,000. (Class 1 railways are those with the most annual revenue. The qualifying amount, $251.4 million in 1995, climbs every year.) By 1989, employment on these American giants was down to 196,000.

As labour costs sank, labour productivity rose. Railways jettisoned excess track, plant and rolling stock; bought advanced computer systems to offer shippers better service than ever before; and by every measure of performance, chalked up spectacular improvements. Freight railways in the U.S., the one nation in which they were all privately owned, became the most efficient in the world. The prices of common shares in U.S. Class 1 railroads zoomed far above the Dow Jones index. Although few Canadians noticed, freight railways blossomed as glamour stocks on U.S. exchanges.

Meanwhile, CN remained hamstrung by government regulations like those its American competitors had so boisterously escaped. As early as 1983, CN and CP claimed the Staggers Act had enabled U.S. competitors to snatch from them traffic worth $100 million. In 1986, with the act still only six years old, the ten most productive American railroads carried, on average, 40 per cent more freight per employee than CN.

CN dared to hope the National Transportation Act (NTA) of 1987 would do for it what the Staggers Act had done for the Americans. The NTA did no such thing. Indeed, it made matters even worse for CN. Canada's new "deregulation" favoured shippers over railways. Why? Canada had thousands of shippers, but only two major railways, one of them a dowdy state enterprise. Shippers were business people with a strong lobby; the Tory government was famously pro-business. In the end, the NTA encouraged competition that led to cuts in the railway freight rates shippers had to pay, but failed to let the railways cut the costs *they* had to pay. It deregulated the price side of the railway business, but not the cost side.

How could CN survive against newly lean, shark-like competition when it carried 90 per cent of its traffic on one third of its trackage, 9 per cent on the second third and an absurd 1 per cent on the last third? An ancient inheritance, CN's grossly underused trackage mostly lay in eastern Canada. By failing to alter regulations that made it notoriously difficult for CN and CP to abandon unprofitable lines, the NTA left a gargantuan problem right where it was: in the railways' lap. As Garth Stevenson explained only a year after Parliament passed the NTA, the legislation exposed CN to more competition "from American railroads, from trucks and even from CP. The abandonment of surplus trackage is not really made any easier, and the problem of actual or potential social obligations is completely ignored. The estimated loss of revenue over a five-year period as a result of the act is in the neighbourhood of one billion dollars."

His estimate proved all too prescient. By 1992, CN and CP had lost $2 billion on their rail operations in eastern Canada. CN's share of this debacle was $1.2 billion. "The railways have experienced an accelerated drop in financial performance since the 1987 NTA was promulgated," a study commissioned by CP and CN concluded in 1992, "with seriously low levels of net income since 1988."

In many obvious ways, CN's achievements remained mighty. As Lawless boasted in 1989, "Every day we handle some 500 freight trains over more than 35,000 kilometres of track, coast to coast in Canada and, through wholly owned subsidiaries, into the northeast and midwest of the United States." Five hundred a day meant more than 182,000 trains per year.

Yet CN often seemed to be languishing in a mature industry serving other mature industries in a mature economy. For at least a century, every improvement in the Canadian economy had seen an increase in the freight the railways carried, but in 1985, even though national output showed healthy growth, CN's freight business declined ominously. Between 1980 and 1991, rail freight traffic in Canada increased by a mere 1 per cent, and the average revenue per ton mile dropped, in real terms, by 35 per cent.

"We must make enough money to pay our taxes, to continue to reduce our long-term debt, and to fund about $450 million in capital needs each year," Lawless said in 1989. Since the recapitalization of 1978, however, CN had never earned a net annual income of anywhere near $450 million. In its best year, 1988, the figure rose only to $283 million. In 1991, as the deepest recession since World War II kept gnawing at the economy, CN's net income showed a *loss* of $14.3 million.

The corporation's revenues were declining faster than it could cut costs. Its return on investment was puny, and its debt once again rising. Moreover, CN was running out of assets to sell off. "Lawless certainly understood things couldn't stay the way they were," says Ronan D. McGrath, CN's former vice-president, information systems and accounting. "Indeed, it was obvious that simply continuing our course would lead to bankruptcy."

With the backing of Lawless, McGrath commissioned what came to be known as "the Kearney report." Among the 1,200 experts at A.T. Kearney Inc., Chicago-based management consultants with thirty-five offices around the world, was Justin F. Zubrod. McGrath ranked him as "the top transportation strategy consultant in the world," and hired him to analyze the marketing, competitive and organizational challenges that CN would have to confront to survive the 1990s. But no matter how superb Zubrod's study might turn out to be, certain CN managers would dismiss it as a made-in-America solution for a made-in-Canada problem. McGrath therefore commissioned a made-in-Canada study as well.

"I told Allan Gregg [president of Decima Research, Toronto] to go out to our customers," he recalled, "and ask where they expected to be in two or three years, where they expected the transportation industry to be, and how these expectations would reflect back on us. How satisfied were they with the CN of 1991, and how fast might that level of satisfaction change?" With the Decima survey in hand, McGrath was ready to argue, "This is not the work of some Yankee expert we've flown in to validate decisions we've already made. This proves our *customers* want change!"

While Zubrod and Gregg were still at work, in October 1991 headlines trumpeted, "CN's own research calls railway bloated," "CN productivity right off the tracks," and "CN's abysmal results build pressure for privatization." Someone had leaked information that would later make an official appearance in the Kearney report. The story turned CN faces red across Canada.

"In an internal study comparing itself with seven major U.S. railways," the *Globe and Mail* reported, "CN found not only that it has substantially more employees than comparable U.S. counterparts but also that its work force has, on average, twice as many administrative workers."

A barrage of equally embarrassing revelations followed:
- Burlington Northern Railroad, Fort Worth, Texas, with 4,000 more miles of track than CN, employed 4,500 fewer administrative workers.
- With respect to revenue ton miles per employee, "a telling snapshot of labour productivity," CN finished "dead last."
- With respect to revenue ton miles per *administrative* employee, CN's performance was even worse, generating less than a third of the American average.

- When researchers used general and administrative expenses to calculate productivity, "CN once again topped the list as least competitive," with expenses of 45 cents for each revenue ton mile per employee, as opposed to the U.S. average of 27 cents.
- In 1990, administrative costs rose $39 million at CN, but at the U.S. lines they dropped an average of $64 million.
- Labour costs consumed 45.6 per cent of every revenue dollar at CN, against an average on the U.S. lines of only 28.1 per cent.

The *Globe*'s story ended with a needle: "CN hauls the largest number of cars per locomotive, an indication that CN's engines may be the hardest working assets the company has."

By early 1992, McGrath had both studies in hand. "I did not give Kearney the Decima work, and I did not give Allan [Gregg] the Kearney work," he recalled, "but there was a *tremendous* degree of convergence. There was scarcely any difference between a marketplace view done by an expert consultant, and a customer view done by an opinion-surveying firm. And that spoke to the quality of both studies."

The Kearney report, which incorporated the most important Decima conclusions, recommended brutal surgery for CN: The elimination, within five years, of 10,000 jobs, and the drastic streamlining of a top-heavy, obsolete, badly focused and excessively layered management structure. Left in place, the report warned, CN's organizational structure would only lead to "further polarization of power among territories, headquarters and regions, resulting in responsibility-accountability confusion, strategy-planning paralysis, proliferation of staff, ineffectiveness in markets, and suboptimization of resources."

CN also required shock therapy to jolt it into an age in which freight railways either gave their customers supreme service—tailor-made for each client, if necessary—or died. "We had to rebuild our technical capabilities to deliver a transportation product," McGrath said. "Customers were demanding more information, much greater reliability and, above all, predictability . . . And if General Motors wanted to be billed by individual vehicle, or if a paper manufacturer wanted to be invoiced on an individual roll, that's what we'd have to be able to do."

Again and again, the Kearney report warned that time was running out for CN: "Customers will not wait for CN—they are more concerned about their own survival . . . Canadian National cannot wait. If the trends of recent years were to continue, CN would be faced with losses in excess of $1 billion annually in four years' time."

If such talk finally awakened the federal government to the gravity of CN's financial crisis, a memo from Lawless to his senior executives, leaked on August 5, 1992, tipped off the whole country. Written in mid-June, two weeks before he retired, the memo predicted CN would lose $100 million in 1992. It reminded the officials that, after a two-day meeting, "we agreed" to cutting 2,000 employees a year for five years; wiping out a third of all management jobs; approaching CP Rail to explore the sharing of shops, yards and track; and, to "dramatize CN's financial situation," putting the CN Tower up for sale.

"The future of CN is at stake," Lawless wrote. "A plan of action for survival is required."

Itching to perfect and implement the plan was the president-and-CEO-in-waiting: Paul M. Tellier.

The Boss
Stirs the Pot

As early as 1990, Paul Tellier told Prime Minister Brian Mulroney he planned to get out of government and into private industry. "He wanted to run his own show," an Ottawa colleague explained, "to prove he could do even more than he did as clerk of the privy council." Tellier was weighing offers in Montreal and Calgary when he learned he was on the short list for Ronald Lawless's job. In his memory, his subsequent conversation with Mulroney went like this:

"Yes, Paul, I would love to see you at CN."

"If I go to CN, Mr. Prime Minister, I'd like to run it on a strictly commercial basis, but I would also like to have a mandate to privatize it."

"Well, you won't be able to pull that off tomorrow morning, but if you turn the situation around, I'll strongly support the privatization of CN."

From the moment Tellier joined the corporation, journalists and union leaders demanded to know if he planned to privatize it. But revealing his goal, he says, would have been "a major technical error." His standard reply was, "My mandate is to turn this company around—as quickly as possible. If my shareholder [the government] wants to privatize the company, he'll let me know in due course."

CN had undeniable strengths. The work force was bloated, but it was also skilled. Moreover, the corporation enjoyed a reputation as a daring innovator in railway technology.

With fine rolling stock and 29,000 kilometres of track, most of it in good shape, CN was the only truly transcontinental railroad in North America. While crossing the mountains of western North America, its grades were less steep, and therefore less costly to ascend, than those of most other lines. Under the St. Clair River, from Sarnia to Port Huron, it was building a two-kilometre, $190-million tunnel—the only link allowing tri-level auto carriers and double-stacked railcars to thunder straight through from central Canada to the American midwest. The tunnel would slash the transit time between Halifax and Chicago by twenty-four hours.

Just before Tellier's arrival, CN had merged its Canadian operations with those of its U.S. subsidiary, the Grand Trunk Corporation (GTC), to form CN North America. The GTC owned the Grand Trunk Western, the Central Vermont, and the Duluth, Winnipeg and Pacific railways. With more than 2400 kilometres of track south of the border, CN North America had access to both the northeastern and midwestern U.S.

"CN has the benefits of the ports of Halifax and Vancouver, two of the deepest and most efficient natural harbours on the continent," Toronto transportation consultant Greg Gormick wrote. "And it has a double-track core system in Ontario and Quebec that thrusts itself into the U.S. market all the way to Chicago, the transportation hub of North America."

Indeed, Gormick insisted CN was "physically and strategically this continent's best railway."

Its most important traffic included coal, sulphur, fertilizers, grain, paper, industrial products, automobiles, auto parts and intermodal freight, and since no single category accounted for more than 20 per cent of its revenues, it boasted the best-balanced mix on the continent. Intermodal freight, which is the cargo that railways carry inside either a truck trailer or a ship container, was the fastest growing part of CN's business.

CN's revenue sources were also varied. Twenty-seven per cent came from offshore export traffic and another 38 per cent from north-south cross-border business. CN carried fully half of Canada's wheat, coal and potash exports, and more than a third of Canadian manufacturers' shipments. With thousands of Canadian shippers facing stiff global competition, CN's ability to maintain low rates and fast, reliable service was crucial to Canada's export trade, and therefore to the health of the national economy.

Yet a whole range of external handicaps—from the crippling regulatory environment to the far higher taxes Canadian railways paid by comparison to U.S. lines—and CN's own flab and sluggishness were threatening to kill it. The corporation's operating ratio showed how unhealthy it was. A crucial gauge of efficiency, the operating ratio shows how many cents a railway spends to earn a dollar. In 1992, when CN was still putting out 97.5 cents for every dollar it collected, the operating ratios of U.S. Class I railways were diving towards the low 80s.

Tellier vowed to make CN's operating ratio plummet in the same way and to do it faster than anyone in CN's old guard thought possible. Every 1 per cent reduction in the ratio would save CN $40 million a year.

Due to start work on October 1, 1992, Tellier arrived on September 30, and told his senior executives to tighten up their five-year business plan. He wanted CN to meet its targets, including the elimination of 11,000 jobs, not within five years, but within three. Vice-presidents who survived Tellier's future executive blood-lettings said he instantly infected the place with an unprecedented sense of urgency. He was a man in a terrible hurry.

He did not, by himself, invent the cures for CN's illness. Many of those had sprung from the Kearney report. "We had much of the basic data nailed down by the time Paul arrived," former vice-president Ronan McGrath explains, "and on September 30, we worked our way through a fair bit of this information." But it was one thing to have information and recommendations, and another to change the world. "We were great at developing plans, but we were terrible at execution," vice-president Jack T. McBain recalls. "Until Paul came along, we just didn't have that relentless push to keep our eye on the ball."

"Tellier brought a huge amount of intensity and focus in moving from the information phase to the execution," McGrath continues, "and that was his greatest contribution. He didn't wait for every 'i' to be dotted and every 't' to be crossed. He moved when there was just enough information to make a decision. And once he'd decided what to do, the debate was fundamentally over. It was going to happen. It was probably going to happen sooner than you'd expect. And there wasn't going to be a whole lot of flexibility."

It was typical of Tellier's in-your-face style that he arranged to meet a dozen CN union leaders on his first day at work.

"I wanted to make a point," he says. "I wanted to tell them I was taking them seriously, but that they should take me seriously, too, because I was determined to turn this place around. The meeting was very high risk, very high risk."

He told the labour leaders exactly what they did not want to hear: The survival of CN would require the disappearance of thousands of union jobs.

"Every guy in the room tried to take a swing at me," he says. "Political patronage, you know! Another goddamn bureaucrat, you know! Appointed to run one of the greatest corporations in the history of Canada, and so on and so forth. It was a rough meeting. It was no love-in. But to this day, I think it was the right move. Some of my executive colleagues were there, and it was a golden opportunity to show them I intended to change a few things."

Two months later, he took spectacular advantage of another such opportunity. He delivered his first public speech as CN's president to the annual dinner of the Toronto Railway Club, a black-tie affair in the cavernous Canadian Room at the Royal York Hotel. CN managers attended by the dozens. Railway executives from across Canada showed up, along with railway union leaders, railway suppliers and railway shippers. The banquet, and the speaker who had worked so intimately with the prime minister, attracted a thousand people.

"That was a speech I wrote myself, personally," Tellier says. "I strongly believe that when you move into any job, you should bring to it a fresh perspective, and it's important to rely on your first impressions."

His perspective on the Canadian railway industry that night sent many railroaders home furious.

"He flayed CN and CP for complacent, ineffective management," Mark Hallman wrote in the *Financial Post*, "and for antediluvian labor practices, male chauvinism, industry inbreeding and inexcusably poor lobbying efforts." Not to mention lousy service.

For Canadian railroads, Tellier charged, customer service remained "more a buzzword than a philosophy we live by." CN and CP were victims of their own primitive attitudes. "If the aerospace, information technology or biotechnology industries modernized at the same stately pace as Canada's railways," the new president of Canada's biggest railway sneered, "we would still be using balloons to forecast weather, storing information on punch cards and proclaiming penicillin a wonder drug."

Working in the Canadian rail industry for little more than two months had already taught him that it maintained "some of the most outdated, old-fashioned labour practices in North America." Tellier damned the century-old payment structures for train crews, the multiplicity of bargaining units, restrictive work regulations, narrow craft rules and rigid seniority customs.

"When I attacked the labour deals, a union leader in the audience shouted, 'Bullshit!' and I took him on," Tellier remembers. "I said, 'No, it is not bullshit, and I'll tell you why it is not bullshit. Name me another industry with such exorbitant labour contracts. Go on. Name me another industry where workers, after eight years on the payroll, can go home and draw full pay until pension time. And management can't even offer them a buyout without you union guys giving your green light.' "

With this one speech, almost a tirade, Tellier told the Canadian railway industry, and especially his own management team, that he would be a force for change like nothing CN had ever seen before. "I have no intention to run CN as a money-losing venture," he vowed. "We will not dally in making the necessary adjustments."

Not surprisingly, shippers liked the speech more than rail executives. "I think Tellier is spot-on," said Maria Rehner, president of the Canadian Industrial Transportation League. Still, she suggested he not repeat the performance because, "If you dump on people from a great height for a long time, as an individual you'll be totally sabotaged."

"He clearly didn't win many friends with that speech," a CP executive said. "A lot of the criticism was correct, sure, but he might now be having difficulties developing a rapport with his new colleagues. He'll have to have that rapport because he sure as hell can't move CN by himself."

Tellier didn't see things that way at all. In his eyes, rapport was to arise not so much from his showing his new colleagues he respected their railway expertise as from their showing *him* they could do the creative and unpalatable things needed to save the corporation.

He was the boss.

CN rumbled along from transaction to transaction, but had no business strategy. With its myriad management layers, overlapping authority, fuzzy lines of command and regional fiefdoms, its structure was a hangover from an era when railways were militaristic within, and lordly without. In both the unions and management, seniority often mattered more than creativity or even efficiency. The imperatives of the mighty operations division no longer totally overrode the interests of customers, but the Decima research revealed shippers were fed up with CN's service: "CN is carrying on a tradition of just going through the motions . . . It's still not customer-focused . . . Dealing with CN is like dealing with bureaucrats . . . They don't even know what competition is . . . They are not aggressive for business."

The uproar over Tellier's not having worked for such a railroad struck him as ironic. It had been railwaymen (with a shove from government, to be sure) who had led CN into its quagmire. So it wasn't another railroader that CN needed, Tellier argued, but a leader, and that's what he would be. He regretted that, too often during his long life in government, he had let colleagues persuade him to move cautiously, that he had suppressed his instinct to push hard for what he knew was right. At last, as commander of CN, he could be *bold*. He could act on his newfound conviction that, "The capacity of any organization to change is unlimited, and the quicker you do it, the better."

He tore into CN's Byzantine hierarchy. "You had a first-line supervisor reporting to a chief," he says, "and the chief reporting to a general manager, the general manager reporting to an assistant vice-president, the assistant vice-president reporting to a vice-president, and the vice-president reporting to a senior vice-president, who reported to the chief executive officer. In some areas, we had twelve levels like this, and the guys on the shop floor told me, 'The message is just not getting through.' "

Tellier imposed on CN "a delayering of authority down to five levels—from me to the first-line supervisors on the shop floor. I was advised to go slow, but this time I followed my own instincts. I told the vice-presidents what I wanted to do and why. Ten weeks later, it was done . . . And to my great surprise, there was no resistance."

Two hundred management positions vanished, "and I told my colleagues, 'If these people can be redeployed, fine, but we've got to flatten the structure.' " McGrath, who received the flattening assignment, says, "I did it very, very quickly, in the late part of '92."

Tellier did not try to convince CN people he knew anything about running railways. "Here is what I bring to this job," he told his new colleagues. "First, I know the shareholder of this company inside out. I know how the government of Canada works, the people within it and how to get decisions from it. Second, I know this country from Newfoundland to British Columbia to the Yukon, and I know all the sensitivities that exist. And third, I have extensive experience in tough negotiations. Negotiations with the provinces, negotiations with the Indians, negotiations with the U.S. I was the deputy minister of energy involved in the deregulation of gas prices with the U.S., and so on.

"So listen, I'm not a railroader, and I'm too old to become one. But *you guys* know railroading. I bring these other things. The complementarity should be extremely good."

It wasn't.

"I discovered very quickly that certain professional railroaders were so fixed in their thinking they just could not accept the amount of change needed," Tellier explains. "They'd say, 'Now Paul, here are seventeen reasons why we cannot do what you want.' So I decided to move them out."

"CN slashes five chairs from executive suite," read a headline in the *Globe and Mail* on January 20, 1993. The immediate savings in salaries would amount to $750,000 a year. Not four months had passed since Tellier's arrival in Montreal. Gone now were Lawless's senior vice-president of operations, and his vice-presidents of quality, legal affairs, and purchasing and materials. Gone, too, were both John Sturgess and his position, chief operating officer. Once a candidate for Tellier's job, Sturgess said philosophically, "This is his [Tellier's] organization. He's reorganizing the company and has eliminated a level of management, namely me."

By so quickly getting rid of management layers and vice-presidents, Tellier showed CN's 33,000 employees that rank-and-file workers would not be the only victims of downsizing. "He gave the signal pretty quickly that *nobody* was indispensable," says Yvon H. Masse, the CN veteran whom Tellier named executive vice-president and chief financial officer in 1993, "and that this business of having a job for life was over. You'd have to earn your keep."

McGrath remembers that, when Tellier arrived, he not only concurred with the Kearney report recommendation that CN cut 10,000 jobs, but added to the future reductions 1,000 jobs from the corporation's U.S. operations. Certain vice-presidents thought Tellier was being too pushy by half. "Nobody was ready to agree that the number should be 11,000, or that we should do it over three years," Tellier says. "The advice I got was 5,000 or 7,000 at best, and don't do it over three years but over five. I decided to ignore the advice, be bold and go for it."

"This was all part of a highly focused effort to make the company privatizable," McGrath says. "As comptroller at the time, I advised Paul we needed a high-key, dramatic announcement about what the downsizing was going to cost us [in severance pay, employment security payments, etc.]. So I proposed we take a $900-million write-off, that we front-load the cost of the work-force reduction into the financials right away . . . So we really front-loaded nearly a billion dollars. We did all this in Paul's first quarter, the last quarter of 1992."

Tellier used these still-secret decisions to avert trouble in New York. "He was effectively summoned there by major bond-rating agencies, which had grown anxious about CN's deteriorating prospects and projections of a $90-million loss on rail operations for 1992," the *Financial Post* reported. "By vowing to make good on plans to slash the work force by 11,000 . . . Tellier was able to keep Standard & Poor's downgrading of CN debt to double A minus from double A. It could have been worse."

In February 1993, Tellier decided he could wait no longer. Cutting CN's work force by a third had been a recommendation, a plan, a rumour, a decision. Time for action. After CN's board of directors warned him the Mulroney cabinet would not stand for his announcing the abolition of 11,000 jobs during an election year, Tellier took what he calls "a Machiavellian step." At a meeting in Montreal, the day before presenting his plan to a cabinet committee in Ottawa, he told CN union leaders what he was about to do. He suspected someone would leak the story, and he was right.

Early on March 1, he awoke at the Chateau Laurier in Ottawa, went for a run on streets he knew better than any in the world, returned to his room, plucked the *Globe and Mail* off the floor and read just what he hoped to read: a front-page story about CN's cutting its work force by 11,000 in three years. "By leaking it," Tellier says, "the unions put it in the public domain."

It was no surprise to him that the cabinet members had all seen the story. "So now they were being asked to make a decision about something that was already on the front page," he continues. "The reaction was, 'Well, Mr. Chairman, we don't like this much, but whether we do it or not, the damage is already done. It's here in the press. And Tellier is right. It should be done, so let's do it.'"

At that same meeting, completing his last days in the federal bureaucracy, was Michael Sabia, the thirty-nine-year-old work addict and deputy secretary of cabinet. Tellier had lured him to CN, and Sabia would shortly arrive there as senior vice-president of corporate development. "He had made the [downsizing] decision internally," Sabia remembers, "and then he pretty skillfully managed Ottawa. He basically took the cards out of Ottawa's hands, because now the hit was there anyway."

Right after the cabinet committee adjourned, Tellier held a press conference to declare that CN would indeed eliminate 11,000 jobs between 1993 and 1995. "The unions started to realize," he says, "that they had an uphill battle on their hands."

No one talked yet about an imminent privatization, but as Sabia says, "That was really when the train left the station. It is *impossible* to overestimate the importance of that decision [to cut 11,000 jobs in three years]. Later, everything flowed out of that."

To put CN on the road to efficiency, Sabia explains, "The Boss [Tellier] had to trash the status quo." The more dramatic the downsizing, the more dramatic the trashing. "The Boss was thinking, 'I need a lever to stir the pot of this organization.' So he reached out for the biggest, roughest, toughest lever he could get his hands on. That really was kind of inspired."

The Wedding
Was Not to Be

"The best professional move Tellier ever made was hiring Michael Sabia," Edward C. Lumley believes. A cabinet minister in the government of Liberal Prime Minister Pierre Trudeau, Lumley was an influential Tellier ally during the events leading up to CN's privatization. "I ate, slept and drank this thing for two and a half years," he says.

Sabia, born in St. Catharines, Ontario, is the son of Dr. Michael Sabia and Laura Sabia, the first president of the National Action Committee on the Status of Women. Michael studied economics and politics at the University of Toronto, completed graduate studies at Yale and walked straight into the federal bureaucracy.

Later, as a senior bureaucrat in the department of finance, Sabia helped design the reviled Goods and Services Tax. "He has an incredibly well-directed, strategic mind," an Ottawa colleague says.

"He gets to the heart of an issue very quickly." Others remembered him as short-tempered on occasion and abrupt with those who disagreed with him. While an assistant secretary and then deputy secretary to the cabinet, Sabia worked with Tellier, but contrary to suspicions in CN's executive suite, they were not chums. "It was a very formal, yes-sir-no-sir kind of relationship," Sabia says.

Remembering the fifteen-hour workdays Sabia put in, Yvon Masse, CN's chief financial officer until he retired in 1995, says, "He is brutal on himself." When a CN employee asked Tellier if he was a workaholic, he replied, "Not me. I'm no Michael Sabia." While Tellier works Sundays at home, Sabia works Sundays at CN headquarters.

"Sabia brought a whole new way of thinking, a whole new dimension to CN," Lumley says. "When he and Paul started at CN, they didn't have too many friends in senior management." With respect to short-lining—selling money-losing stretches of track to smaller operators with lower costs—"all these regional barons and some of the other senior managers were just totally bucking Paul and Michael. CN wasn't used to somebody with a strategic mind, and Michael is a brilliant strategist."

As vice-president, corporate development, Sabia helped change CN's management culture. He imposed on the company financial standards and controls like those at major Canadian and U.S. corporations. But back in the spring and summer of 1993, he says, "I was still just trying to slice and dice the business. I spent a lot of time taking the East apart from the West, and working out scenarios for recovery in the East. The first inescapable conclusion was that we *had* to fix the East. We were very deep in the tank in the East."

In the years 1988–93, CN and CP together racked up losses of more than $2 billion on their operations east of Winnipeg. The problem, as Tellier described it, was this: "Too many cars, with too many employees and too many miles of track, are chasing too few freight dollars." Three transcontinental lines, each costly to maintain, crossed northern Ontario, which generated little freight. In parts of southern Ontario, parallel CP and CN tracks lay not 20 metres apart. CN alone had more than 13,000 kilometres of track between Winnipeg and Halifax, enough to span Canada twice.

In the East, where the railways hauled goods ranging from pulp and paper to auto parts to beer, both companies had long taken a fierce beating from trucks. The huge highway network in central Canada, the low labour costs in trucking and the nature of the traffic—mostly manufactured goods on short runs—all gave the trucking industry an enormous advantage.

For hauling traffic like grain, coal and sulphur over long distances, freight trains are unbeatable, which is why CN and CP were profitable in the West. But CN's eastern losses threatened its western business. For example, Japan could get cheap coal from Australia, but CN's losses in the East prevented it from reducing its charges in the West for shipping coal to Pacific Rim ports. "Let's face it," Tellier said. "Westerners have been subsidizing rail services in eastern Canada for quite a while."

Two of his shrewdest consultants, Lumley and business executive Torrance J. Wylie—a former director of the federal Liberal party and political adviser to prime ministers Lester Pearson and Pierre Trudeau—argued that salvation for CN lay in cooperating with CP to clean up their shared mess in the East. Cost-cutting and short-lining were important, to be sure, but if Tellier relied on those alone, Lumley warned, "Five years from now, you'll still be farting around, and you won't be any further ahead on the bottom line. You'll be spending five years just looking over your shoulder—cut, cut, cut—instead of trying to grow the business."

Historically, CP had taken the initiative in proposing some variety of merger or takeover to solve the crown corporation's financial problems, but this time CN's boss called on CP's.

"I went to Stinson [William Stinson, chairman and chief executive officer of Canadian Pacific]," Tellier recalls, "and I said to him, 'You're losing your shirt in the East and so are we. Why don't we see what we can do together? You have a big opportunity here because

I don't belong to this railway culture. I have no lifelong loyalty to CN. I don't come from there. All that matters to me is the bottom line.' And this led to some discussions."

More than a year later, after Sabia had immersed himself in the talks with CP Rail, Tellier revealed the fruit of the discussions. "Canada's two railways want to end their historic rivalry and merge their entire operations east of Winnipeg [later Thunder Bay] to staunch the financial bleeding that has weakened both," a Canadian Press story explained on December 23, 1993. "CN North America and CP Rail would ask the government for permission to pool their eastern assets in a new system. The new railway, which senior executives have dubbed Newco in their top-secret talks, could be operational as early as January 1996."

Newco would be Canada's third major railroad, the only one whose territory would extend from Thunder Bay down to Halifax. CN and CP would continue to compete in the West. They would share Newco's ownership and manage it at arm's length. "CN's relationship to it," Tellier says, "was going to be much the same as our relationship to two American railroads, Conrail and Burlington Northern."

Instantly attacked by unions who feared layoffs and by shippers who feared a railway monopoly, Tellier's revelations inspired the Vancouver *Sun* to call him "the National Dream-buster." They also caught CP off guard. CP officials insisted a merger was only one of several ideas under study, but finally, on January 12, 1994, Stinson said a full merger of the two systems in the East was "the preferred option." Indeed, he added, "This is one heck of an opportunity to put together a very strong railroad industry."

Not a month passed before transport minister Doug Young approved a continuation of the talks. CN and CP expected that, come springtime, they would show the government a detailed agreement in principle.

This was a new government. Led by Jean Chrétien, the Liberals had driven the Tories from power the previous October. As the boss of CN, Tellier was now answering to a Liberal transport minister for the first time. A headline in the *Financial Post* had trumpeted, "Paul Tellier brings his damn-the-torpedoes style to long-suffering CN." By February 1994, Doug Young, the most driven and least diplomatic of the freshmen cabinet ministers, was already bringing his own damn-the-torpedoes style to the transport department. Relations between Tellier and Young would not always be harmonious.

During the first half of 1994, Tellier periodically met the chairman and chief executive of CP Rail System, Barry Scott, while Sabia did the day-to-day haggling for CN. Indeed, Sabia and CP officials had been carrying on secret negotiations since the previous fall. As the talks continued in 1994—mostly between him and Katharine Braid, executive vice-president of CP Rail—he drew on the expertise of the CN executives he trusted, A. T. Kearney Inc., New York investment bankers Morgan Stanley & Co., Inc. and Toronto investment bankers Burns Fry Ltd.

Burns Fry was a relatively new CN ally. The venerable Scotia-McLeod Inc. had long been the railway's Canadian adviser on financial matters, but Sabia believed they had become "far too comfortable. They thought they owned us, so we switched. It was a matter of stirring the pot again, right? Dump Scotia, bring in Burns."

When the merger workload became intolerable, even for a Sabia, he hired Claude Mongeau, a hard-driving young executive at Imasco Ltd. as assistant vice-president, corporate development. If Sabia was Tellier's first lieutenant, Mongeau was Sabia's. Mongeau, too, was the antithesis of a clock-watcher.

Jeff Ward of A. T. Kearney, the consulting firm, was another invaluable contributor to Sabia's preparations for the merger talks. "Jeff worked till he could hardly see," Sabia recalls. "Claude was my right-hand man in those days, and Jeff was my left-hand man."

The merger negotiations were among the most complicated in the business history of Canada. Would CN control Newco, or would CP? What about the value and allocation of assets? How much of

CP's and CN's American freight operations would be part of the deal? How would Newco relate to its parent companies with respect to daily operations? How would CN and CP marry their rival administrative and marketing operations in the East? What would Newco's management structure be like? How many CN and CP workers would the merger affect? What lines, yards, shops and rolling stock would vanish or be short-lined? And what, exactly, would Newco's territory be?

Aware that unions, shippers and dozens of railway towns in Ontario were at best suspicious of the merger, and at worst reviled it, both Tellier and CP executives kept sounding alarms about the terrible plight of their lines. "Too few Canadians realize that their nation's railways face a grave and immediate crisis," Tellier said. CP's William Stinson warned that, if government refused to endorse the merger, CN and CP would lose so badly to trucks that "Canada would have to undertake massive new highway construction."

"Either we cut our losses in the East or we will stop investing," Tellier declared. "If we stop investing, the quality of our service will go down. There will be more derailments. We will have to run our trains at a lower speed."

He told a parliamentary committee that in 1993, CN had lost $200 million on its eastern operations and had seen its long-term debt soar to $2.3 billion. Unrealistic labour costs, he argued, were killing CN. On average, weekly wages for CN union members were $300 higher than the wages trucking firms paid. "He also cited work rules 'dating from the last century,' which led to systematic overstaffing," the Montreal *Gazette* reported, "and required the railway to continue to pay as many as 700 people who no longer worked for the company."

"If the merger is delayed," Tellier warned members of Parliament, "five years from now the situation could be such that some kind of bailout [the first since the 1970s] would be required." Then he told the Canadian Club in Montreal, "Unless we correct the situation, our losses will grow to $1.5 billion by 1997."

In speech after speech, Tellier hammered home these points:

- To respond properly to the demands of shippers, CN had no choice but to make enormous investments in superior technology, yet it wasn't coming even close to earning its cost of capital.
- Canada's regulatory system was so archaic that abandoning or short-lining unprofitable trackage took months, and sometimes years, with the meter running. U.S. competitors thrived in a far more streamlined environment.
- CN paid $293 million in fuel, property and income taxes in 1993, but if it had operated exclusively in the U.S., the bill would have been $125 million lower. A train running from Vancouver to Toronto cost $10,000 more in taxes than a train running from Seattle to Chicago.
- CN's revenue per ton mile, per employee, remained 70 per cent below the average on U.S. railroads. (In labour productivity, the Montreal *Gazette* reported, both CN and CP had "a dreadful record.")
- Whereas CN had to pay for the construction and maintenance of its lines, the public financed the roads and highways that trucks used. (On this point, Harry Gow of the Ottawa-based consumer group Transport 2000 said, "The railways are helping pay for the deficit, highways and airports, but they are getting damn little help themselves.")
- As freer trade forced the integration of the Canadian and American economies, transportation flow was shifting to a north-south axis. CN therefore faced increasingly fierce competition from U.S. railroads, the most efficient in the world. (Most Asian freight bound for central Canada arrived at Seattle. U.S. railways hauled it to Chicago and then north into Canada, robbing CN and CP of revenue.)

In defence of the merger, Tellier said, it was at last time "to abandon the unproductive symbolism that made the railway a kind of monument to the past that was not to be touched."

The merger talks flowed so smoothly for three months that Stinson and Tellier expected to show the government an agreement in May, but the negotiations dragged on until mid-July. The stalemate involved a disagreement over the value of CN's eastern assets.

"Stinson said, and Barry Scott repeated it, 'We've got to run this 50-50,' " Tellier remembers. "And I said, 'Listen, we are much bigger than you in the East, so it can't be 50-50.' So then they said, 'Okay, we will compensate you accordingly.' We had reached an agreement on just about everything except this key point: How much would they give us to reflect the fact that we were much bigger than them?"

Tellier wanted $650 million. Barry Scott, the boss at CP Rail, offered $500 million. But Scott also wanted to include in the deal CP's money-losing Delaware and Hudson Railway. "I felt Canadian taxpayers couldn't afford to make such a gift to CP shareholders," Tellier explains. "I said, 'Listen, if the D&H makes money, fine. If it doesn't, you pick up the tab.' "

At a tense and uncompromising meeting near the end of July, Tellier remembers, "I drew the bottom line. I said, 'I'll make a deal at $575 million, but if you want the D&H in it, you'll have to pay for it.' " Scott disliked the location of Tellier's bottom line, but they agreed to meet in CP's boardroom the next morning.

When Tellier showed up, Scott shocked him. He handed him a letter that not only broke off the negotiations, but proposed that CP Rail buy all of CN's operations east of Thunder Bay and Chicago. Although the gap in asset evaluation was the chief reason CP cancelled the talks, Scott also referred to "some twist towards the end. We felt CN wasn't completely up-front in some aspects of the detail that was necessary for both parties to come to an agreement. That did colour things."

Tellier was less mysterious: "I don't think real negotiations ever took place. This went on far too long."

"Paul Tellier felt he'd been deceived," says Evan Siddall, a member of the Burns Fry (later Nesbitt Burns) team of CN advisers. "He had bargained in good faith, and our suspicion was that CP, all along, had merely been trying to suck confidential information out of CN before trying to buy its eastern operations."

Some CN executives shared this suspicion, but two years after the anger of July 1994 had subsided, Tellier and Sabia dismissed the theory. They believed CP had done its sincere best to strike a fair deal. "I give them the benefit of the doubt," Tellier says.

Sabia suspects the real reason for the collapse of the negotiations was older than the negotiators. "There's just an enormous amount of bad history between these two companies," he says. "I still see it every day. People who've been here a long time always look for the worst in CP. A number of people here thought we should just have a good go at them, and try to take them out of business. That was a view I never shared. I still don't. But you know, there was just a lot of baggage. It goes back generations. There are guys in this company today—and they are good guys—who would rather die than do anything mutually beneficial with CP. I think that's true on the other side, too."

CP executives, Sabia continued, simply could not see CN as anything but "that same old, bloated corporation." To them, hell would freeze over before he and Tellier, a pair of railway know-nothings from the federal bureaucracy, achieved a turnaround at CN. "They looked at us with that typical railroader arrogance," Sabia continues. "And you know, it was the most marvellous kind of arrogance because, my God, you looked at the condition of CP and CN, and what was there to be arrogant about?"

CN's brutal work-force reductions would affect the amount of operating income it could bring to Newco, "and that of course was key in sorting out the financial arrangements." During his months of negotiations with Katharine Braid, however, Sabia sensed that no one at CP, from Stinson and Scott on down, believed CN would meet its cost-cutting targets.

"It was hard for them to acknowledge that—God, you know— that company we've been looking down on for generations may even have stolen a step on us," Sabia adds. "Our perception was: 'We are doing it and we're going to be paid for it.' Their perception was: 'No, you haven't done it, you'll never do it and we're not going to pay you for it.' And at the end of the day, that's why the thing pulled apart."

Finally, CN's health was looking up. Its need for the merger was no longer quite as desperate as it had been six months earlier. This may have influenced Tellier when he was drawing his bottom line for Scott. Just two days later, he said, "I wouldn't be surprised to see CN turn a profit of $150 million this year, after a loss of $75 million in 1993." The turnaround was under way, and though no one knew it yet, CP's abrupt cancellation of the merger talks had shoved its historic rival onto a fast track to privatization.

Fitness Program
for a Railway

Sixteen months after Paul Tellier quit government to join CN, he blasted federal civil servants in a speech to the Canadian Institute in Ottawa. Their jobs, he told them, were "not to maintain some towering bureaucracy," but to serve the Canadian people. Their record in abolishing useless programs was "far from spectacular." Life at CN had already taught him that "no major downsizing or significant re-engineering process will be effective if implemented slowly and timidly."

The federal bureaucracy's classification system, with sixty occupation groups, was "outdated, inefficient, complex and cumbersome." The Privy Council Office had once had a plan for "a radical, bold and rapid change" of this system, and "I deplore letting some of my former colleagues persuade me to go slow." The gradual approach had achieved only "very small, modest changes . . . We still have a system where senior managers hire consultants to write ten-page job descriptions that nobody reads!"

Then came the crusher: "I have implemented more change in the last twelve months at CN than I was able to achieve in my last seven years in the public service."

A few months later, Tellier said he was leading nothing less than "the most ambitious program of change and renewal ever in the history of Canadian railways." His resolve crackled in the air during every meeting of CN brass. One vice-president says Tellier often opened a discussion by announcing a plan, and then as he described it, grew more and more passionate. "Maybe ten minutes would pass," the executive said, "before anyone else uttered a word."

No change was more drastic—or painful—than the reduction of the work force by 11,000 in three years.

To coordinate the job-slashing, Tellier appointed CN veteran Ronan McGrath, then vice-president, information systems and accounting. Even before the end of 1992, which was two months before the cabinet knew the downsizing schedule, McGrath set up an administrative unit with a faintly Orwellian name: the Program Control Centre. Its job, he says, was "to measure every job and every plan in the corporation to get staffing out."

The work, McGrath remembers, was "the toughest possible. The choices were stark, but it had to be done. CN was like a lifeboat. You could keep it overcrowded and sink it, or you could make sure you had only enough people aboard to keep it afloat."

Tellier, he continues, "drove this to a high degree of intensity. There were a lot of very, very tough meetings. If you missed a target in one area, you had to find it in another. And if we started to go off target, there was visible tension in the room when the report went in, which was monthly."

Although the first purpose of the drastic surgery was to cut costs, an unexpected benefit emerged. Every month, Michael Sabia says, Tellier declared, "Look, we're gonna hit this number." If an executive said he couldn't possibly hit the number, he would be told, "Change the way you're doing the work to hit the number, because the number is going to be met."

"Now that led the good managers to redesign the way they did the work," Sabia says, "and we discovered tremendously new ways to run the business. Whether it was in track maintenance, or the operation of our locomotive fleet, all across the board, The Boss had forced people to say, 'Well, we can't do X as we've always done it—because we won't have the people anymore if we hit the number—so we've got to change how we do X.'

"From a senior manager's perspective, it also showed us who the really good managers *were*. Who were the guys reinventing the way they did the work, and who were the guys just stripping bodies off? So as we got into it, we saw that this thing was just an amazing driver of creativity. It separated the wheat from the chaff. Who could do it? Who couldn't? And that led to a whole bunch of people changes, which stimulated another round of change. So it's impossible to overestimate the importance of that [downsizing] decision. I don't think anybody, including The Boss, understood at first the sheer magnitude of its importance. It set the table for so much that followed."

Between November 6, 1992, five weeks after Tellier became The Boss, and January 27, 1994, a total of 4,100 CN jobs vanished.

He envisaged a revolution in the freight industry. With the Canadian, American and Mexican economies becoming more and more interdependent, Tellier predicted competition for sales would occur among regions, not just companies. Transportation would become crucially important to the economies of these regions. To deliver supreme service, trains and trucks would have to compete against each other less and cooperate with each other more. Railways would have to exploit the most advanced technologies to offer unheard-of flexibility and reliability, up-to-the-minute information on the location of shipments and, to spare customers inventory costs, just-in-time delivery.

"Freight trains will have fixed dates and fixed times of departure, and an estimated time of arrival as reliable as airlines enjoy," Tellier told a truckers' conference. "You will be able to ship and receive with the same degree of certainty as when you pick someone up at the airport." Even if a container moved by ship, railway and truck, the system would produce only "one electronic instruction, one bill for services rendered." This "seamless transportation" would spread throughout all three North American nations.

By late 1993, CN had working alliances with major American railways, as well as trucking firms in the U.S. and across Canada. In a further move to avoid languishing in the exhaust fumes of the revolution, it was spending $100 million to install its own version of the industry's most sophisticated freight management system, the Service Reliability Strategy.

Despite the corporation's reputation for being stodgy and sluggish, it had in fact been a technology pioneer. But competitors complained that CN, unlike them, could always rely on the federal treasury to finance its costly research and development. CN bore the eternal curse of the crown corporation. If it spent too little on renewing physical capital, it was damned for backwardness; if it spent too much, it was damned both for extravagance and for driving private industries to the wall. Whatever the truth of such accusations, CN was the North American leader in the technologies of concrete ties, continuous welded rail and wayside detectors that measured the impact of wheels as they rolled over rails. By 1993, it boasted the world's most advanced Operations Management Centre, which enabled staff to foresee and prevent problems up to twenty-four hours ahead, all across a vast track network.

CN also invented the BELTPACK, one of the most important contributions to railway technology since the diesel engine. No bigger than a lunch pail, the BELTPACK has a radio link to a computer in a locomotive cab. Holding the device at waist height and flicking the right switches, ground workers operate driverless yard engines to make up trains. Yard locomotives weigh up to 137,000 kilograms, yet deft BELTPACK operators can force them to couple cars gently, quickly and safely. Each BELTPACK replaces up to four highly paid yard engineers, freeing them for duty in main-line locomotives. By late 1996, CN yards would boast 105 BELTPACKs, reducing the railway's annual labour bill by $24 million. The corporation's consulting arm, CANAC International Inc., had begun to sell the boxes all over the continent.

The Service Reliability Strategy (SRS), though not a CN invention, would enable the railway to serve shippers as it never had before. Like other railroads, CN had traditionally managed *trains*, not individual shipments. Shippers, however, had become so demanding that the most competitive railways had installed systems to reveal the precise service requirements for each carload, the final destination, the promised time of delivery, and at all times during the shipment, the carload's location. It was now possible to determine if a shipment was on schedule, behind schedule or ahead. "In today's marketplace, that shipment-management capability is what you've got to have," says Gerald Davies, who worked for Class 1 American railroads before joining CN as senior vice-president, marketing. "It's absolutely essential."

As CN boasted, the implementation of its SRS was "one of the largest single business-technology re-engineering projects in North American railway history." The Kearney report had recommended CN improve service by entirely rebuilding its computer systems, and Tellier agreed the moment he arrived. "So we went ahead," Ronan McGrath says, "and we bought the SRS from the Santa Fe, then the best railway in the world."

Adapting the SRS to CN's requirements was indeed a colossal task. "There were 10 million lines of computer code, and we had to retrain 10,000 people," McGrath continues. "The SRS affects our billing, our transportation management, our yards, our fleet planning. It's very much what runs the whole corporation. The task was technically daunting but, more important, it involved a huge process change. Paul gave us just three years. With no outs. And a budget of $100 million. No outs on that, either. We just had to do it, and we did. And it moved CN from being at the tail end of the railway industry, to being a leader in this kind of technology. Today, CN's traffic-management system is among the very best in the business."

CN has gigantic customers. Indeed, its top 800 clients account for 97 per cent of its revenue, and the *average* deal CN sales staff strike with a customer brings in some $3.5 million per year. Some deals are worth hundreds of millions.

With stakes that high, Tellier sought to invigorate and revamp CN's unwieldy and poorly focused marketing operation. The corporation, he believed, "wasn't all that good at finding out what its customers wanted and was even less capable of changing its ways to deliver the desired service." So he hired Gerald Davies. It would be Davies's job to teach CN's marketing staff to serve shippers as well as or better than the best U.S. railroads.

Davies arrived in November 1993. He had been a marketing vice-president for Burlington Northern Railroad (annual revenue when he was there: about US$5 billion) and also for CSX Transportation (US$4.6 billion). At CSX, he had learned firsthand how indispensable an SRS was. As another CSX executive, Alex Mandl, said in Alvin Toffler's *Power Shift*, "It's not enough just to deliver products. Customers want information. Where their products will be consolidated and deconsolidated, what time each item will be where, prices, customs information, and much more. We are an information-driven business."

"CN's marketing was very fragmented when I arrived," Davies says. The reason was ancient. At freight railways, the operations brass, not marketing executives, traditionally had the whip hand. This virtually guaranteed customer service would not be the top priority. When Mike Walsh became CEO of the Union Pacific Railroad in 1986, he said later, it was focused on "how to run the trains efficiently rather than how to serve the customer's needs . . . If you had only fifty cars today, you just waited until tomorrow or the next day when you had a hundred. It built up tonnage and it saved fuel, but it drove our customers up the wall."

At CN, Davies quickly discovered, "The marketing staff were reporting to the regional operations chiefs. So we completely restructured that whole marketing function and brought it all into just six business units." The units, which each earned annual revenue of at least $400 million, were: Grain and Grain Products; Coal, Sulphur and Fertilizer; Intermodal; Industrial Products; Forest Products; and Automotive.

Another marketing weakness at CN, Davies says, lay in the staff's poor grasp of "what the marketplace was like, what the opportunities were and where the challenges lay. These people were dedicated, but they just weren't properly organized and focused. So again, we changed all that around. We put market specialists in place. Their job was to tell us where the various segments of our marketplace were headed and how to position ourselves to capitalize on opportunities."

Finally, CN marketers didn't understand CN customers. "We were intensely focused on each transaction," Davies says, "but not at all on where that account was headed, or on what customers needed from us to succeed in their own marketplaces." He therefore established a system of account managers. Each big customer got an account manager exclusively to itself. "We have one account manager for General Motors, for example, and he has to understand everything that's going on there, whether it affects us or not," says Davies. "He must also present us to GM so they understand how *we* can add value to *their* process. Our account managers are responsible for the profitability of our accounts, and for these customers' levels of loyalty to CN and satisfaction with our service . . . They have to make sure we're doing the right things, the right way, the right time, every time."

The drive to please shippers included a radical streamlining of customer services. CN had nineteen of what it called "existing service units"—including major "customer management activities" in Edmonton, Toronto, Montreal and Moncton—but in 1994 it started to consolidate all these in Winnipeg. This would give customers round-the-clock service from a single point of contact.

Choosing a team to whip CN into shape, Tellier not only imported railway professionals like Davies (and discarded vice-presidential deadwood), he also identified CN veterans who had become his invaluable allies. These included Alphonse Giard, vice-president, legal affairs and corporate secretary, and Yvon H. Masse, executive vice-president and chief financial officer. A trim, courteous gentleman with neat, white hair, Masse had been at CN thirty-one years when Tellier ordered him and his colleagues to do in three years what they had planned to do in five. The old-timer and the newcomer clicked.

"Yvon would say to me, 'Paul, this is new to me, but if you want to do it, we'll try,' " Tellier recalls. "He was not the youngest one, but he had an open mind."

In 1994, Masse arranged for one of CN's U.S. subsidiaries to issue and sell auction preferred stock for US$200 million, mostly to finance construction of CN's tunnel under the St. Clair River. That same year, in just one week, he persuaded Salomon Brothers Inc., New York, to buy CN 7 per cent notes worth US$300 million.

"We wanted to put on our balance sheets funds at lower rates," Masse explains. "We used the low end of the cycle, and the timing was good. This financing gave us peace while negotiating with CP and, later, while undertaking the privatization. We didn't have to go back to the markets. If you had go to the market for a substantial sum while talking about rationalizing or privatizing, you'd have paid a premium."

Masse's shrewd moves and canny timing during the sale of subsidiaries resulted in CN windfalls worth tens of millions.

Another member of the old guard who sprang eagerly into Tellier's new and rushing order was chief engineer John (Jack) McBain. The new CEO had been on the job only three months when he promoted McBain to senior vice-president, operations. McBain had joined the engineering department in 1965, and Tellier and Sabia consider him a prime example of an old hand whose creativity blossomed under the heat and pressure of slashing costs.

"I was a frustrated manager in the old organization," McBain says. "I felt shackled by the crown corporation mentality. But when Paul Tellier came in, he was saying, 'Don't let any of the traditional decisions get in your way. You now have the freedom to develop whatever initiatives you think will move us forward.' "

McBain urged "a dramatic change in the philosophy for maintaining our fleet." Traditionally, CN had kept locomotives alive with a ceaseless round of overhauls. The railway was forever remanufacturing ancient locomotives. "It was costing us a fortune to keep this old fleet in reliable, high-quality condition," McBain says. "So we did all the necessary analysis to convince our board that, rather than go on in that old and expensive way, we should buy new."

That's exactly what CN chose to do, and its decision led to a locomotive deal worth $300 million, the biggest in Canadian history. From the diesel division of General Motors of Canada, CN ordered 105 4,300-horsepower locomotives, all spanking new and all more fuel efficient than the ones they replaced. That was only the beginning. The corporation planned to buy nearly 300 more new and highly productive locomotives over the next fifteen years.

McBain also found better ways to maintain both fleet and track. CN had always used its own workers and supervisors to look after locomotives, but now it brought General Motors managers into its shops in Toronto and Edmonton. "So we're still using CN employees," McBain says, "but we're also using the production-line skills of the manufacturers to provide efficient maintenance for more than 500 locomotives."

In 1994, McBain's second full year as a senior vice-president, CN so streamlined its methods of looking after trackage that, even while improving and accelerating the work, it closed shops and eliminated more than 700 maintenance jobs.

The hacking, the paring, the driving-out of cost, and the feverish search for better but cheaper ways to perform continued in every corner of CN—before, during and after CP called off the merger talks. "In every sector where they could get some cost savings, these two ex-bureaucrats, Tellier and Sabia, identified them," Torrance Wylie explains, "and then went after them. Relentlessly and fearlessly. So that all during this debate about the future of CN, they were taking huge steps every month to improve its cost basis. They went into areas where the corporation had temporized for years."

Privatization
Builds Up Steam

When CP halted its merger negotiations with CN in July 1994 and offered to buy CN East, the chairman of the crown corporation, Brian Smith, said, "I'm surprised and disappointed because I thought a deal was there." Since CN was bigger than CP, he added, "The mouse is offering to buy the elephant." Rail experts said the government's approving such a buyout, which might well have devastated dozens of small towns and caused thousands of layoffs, would be political suicide. "A government willing to risk this," said John Gratwick, a railway consultant in Halifax, "would also be willing to risk an armed insurrection from within."

CP's retreat from the negotiations, however, left CN dangling. The crown corporation still had no solution to its mess in the East. Where would it go from here? Privatization had been in the backs of several minds, including Paul Tellier's, but few thought it would happen within five years. Now, in August 1994, he and Torrance Wylie, as well as CN's financial advisers, Nesbitt Burns Inc., began to talk more seriously about the issue. If the government was considering selling part of CN to CP, shouldn't it consider selling *all* of it to private investors? Edward Lumley, vice-chairman of Nesbitt Burns, kicked the idea around with transport minister Douglas Young.

Even before CP revealed how much it would pay for CN's eastern operations, the *Financial Post* reported that "CN's politically savvy chief executive, who will influence the government's final decision, is said to have told his executives CN East is not for sale." Although privatizing CN would be the government's decision, not Tellier's, he nevertheless said it was "surely one of the options that has to be examined."

On Thursday, September 22, CP offered $1.4 billion for CN East, but attached so many strings to the deal that CN consultants from Morgan Stanley Group Inc., put its economic value at "zero or even negative." David McLean, the Vancouver lawyer and businessman whom Prime Minister Jean Chrétien was about to name chairman of CN, said later the CP offer would actually have *cost* CN anywhere from $200 million to $400 million.

"The $1.4 billion was window dressing, not real money," Tellier says. "I'll give you an example in plain English. I say to you, 'I want to buy your house. I'll give you $200,000 for it, but of course I'm assuming there's a car in the garage, and it's got to be a new model. I'm assuming there's a big freezer in the basement, and you've filled it to capacity with fine food. And, oh yes, I'm assuming you'll persuade your neighbour to move his fence because I want to build a swimming pool.' " In the CP offer, the equivalents to the car, food, freezer and boundary change lay in CN's receivables and inventories, and in its getting a ruling to enable CP to exploit CN's accumulation of tax losses. "So in the end," Tellier says, "they would not be paying anything to acquire CN East, but it was very skillfully done."

The offer struck some of his confidants as ludicrous, and others as insulting. "Paul went up the wall when he got it," Torrance Wylie recalls, "but I said, 'Paul, this is just wonderful! It's a godsend. This is just so bad it's going to self-destruct. It has no credibility anywhere. So you don't have to spend a whole lot of time explaining why it's inadequate. And there's no need to take a haircut [from CP] when you can get much more in the marketplace. Now we've got to get on with taking the company to the *real* potential buyers, and they're in the public marketplace.' "

Looking back, Michael Sabia believes the collapse of the merger talks and the absurd CP bid for CN East showed all Canada the plight of its railway industry. These were unintentional but supremely effective ways to broadcast the "what's-here-today-won't-work-tomorrow-message." So what *would* work tomorrow?

"It all sounds pretty neat now," Sabia continues, "and wouldn't it be wonderful if we could claim we said, 'Yeah, here's how we'll do it. First, we'll announce the abolition of 11,000 jobs, and then we'll talk about a merger with CP in the East, and then the merger talks will collapse, and CP will try to buy us out, and we'll do this and that, and we'll pull off this *terrific* privatization'? It would be great to be able to say we planned every step, but of course we didn't."

The government did not formally reject CP's offer for several weeks, but on September 30, transport minister Young assigned a task force of nine parliamentarians to hold hearings across Canada on the possibilities for "the commercialization" of CN. (The Liberals, Sabia says, "had been elected to repudiate everything the previous government had done," and in 1994 "still couldn't even speak the word 'privatization.' They used 'commercialization,' whatever that was!") The *Financial Post* called the appointment of the task force "a major step toward possible privatization of Canada's largest crown corporation."

At 7 P.M. on October 3, Tellier, Young and Lumley met over a light dinner in the Nesbitt Burns boardroom in the financial heart of Toronto. This meeting, too, was a major step towards CN's privatization. "Can we do it?" Young asked. The answer from Lumley and Tellier was, "Yes, sir." Lumley, however, warned Young, "It won't be easy. There are a whole lot of obstacles to overcome. The biggest thing is that Paul has to meet his targets, and that means you, Mr. Minister, will have to stand behind him."

On the evening of the Tellier-Young-Lumley dinner, not a year had passed since Prime Minister Chrétien had named Meredith Edward Douglas Young, fifty-four, his minister of transport. Yet the fluently bilingual, self-made millionaire from Tracadie, an Acadian town in an impoverished corner of northern New Brunswick, was already known as a tough, pushy, bullying and efficient cabinet minister. Chrétien made other ministers aware that he ranked Young as an ace at getting hard jobs done well.

Young, the *Globe and Mail* reported, "was known to have interrupted hand-wringing cabinet ministers to remind them they have their marching orders from the Prime Minister's Office, so why don't they just save their breath and get on with the task at hand." According to the *Toronto Star*, "Young is the Dirty Harry of Chrétien's cabinet and proud of his 'Go ahead, make my day' attitude."

"Doug Young is a tough SOB," a New Brunswick acquaintance allowed. "He likes dismantling or building things. It doesn't really matter which to him. As long as he's doing something."

What Young was aiming to dismantle in 1994 was most of his own department. He was out to reshape not just the rail industry, but Canada's entire transportation system. "Transportation is an absolutely essential component of a nation's competitiveness," he said. "If we can't get it right, we're going to pay a hell of a price." In his opinion, Canada had not yet got it right, and much of what was wrong with it lay in a flabby Transport Canada. "Doug Young has been called Canada's most revolutionary transport minister," the *Journal of Commerce* reported. "He has also been called a sabre-rattling reformer who has bitten off more than he can chew. What he has bitten off is a commercialization concept where up to 75 per cent of Transport Canada is destined for transfer to private industry or nonprofit organizations."

The transfers were to include ports, airports, air-traffic control systems, some Coast Guard services and the St. Lawrence Seaway. "With almost messianic zeal," the *Journal* reported, Young was planning the elimination of grain-shipping subsidies worth hundreds of millions of dollars, and three quarters of Transport Canada's work force and budget. Asked why he moved with such ruthless speed, Young said he had no illusions about longevity in Canadian political life, "nor time for all the niceties. That's why I am not expecting a diplomatic posting."

But his plan included more than just the swift reduction of Transport Canada. For CP and CN, he promised a thorough reform of the regulatory system that handicapped them in the struggle against U.S. competitors. In the fall of 1995, that pledge would help sell CN shares to gigantic institutional investors. In the fall of 1994, however, few of Young's associates believed the shares would ever sell to anyone.

"When I talked about [privatizing CN] for the first time, even in a semi-formal way," he says, "everybody, practically without exception, burst out laughing. And some of my esteemed colleagues ventured the thought that they wouldn't put a buck in it, so why would anybody else? Others wondered whether or not the government would end up with a buck—or would it actually cost us *more* to privatize it because we'd have to deal with the debt load and all the rest of it? So it wasn't exactly met with great enthusiasm."

Young's parliamentary task force visited twelve cities in nine provinces, considered more than 160 submissions, and heard the representatives of cities, towns, unions, pensioners, shippers, port authorities, industrial commissions, provincial governments, the grain, forest and chemical industries, and, indeed, every interest group from Sioux Lookout Economic Development to the Canadian Fertilizer Institute. Just before the MPs hit the road, they got a quick education in Canadian rail economics from Tellier and other CN executives, A. T. Kearney, Nesbitt Burns, Transport Canada and the National Transportation Agency. Robert Nault, chairman of the task force and Liberal MP for Kenora-Rainy River, Ontario, also made sure the group had a private meeting with "the major players in the unions."

The beauty of Nault's appointment was that nobody could say he was in CN's back pocket. A former CP conductor who might one day return to the railway, he had been a negotiator for the United Transportation Union. Young's choice of Nault to run the task force, Tellier says, was "a brilliant move, a brilliant move." Nault knew the railway business, had credibility with the unions and understood the transport minister. "Yeah, we get along very well," Young says. "Nault's tough as nails. He's no patsy." Informed that Nault felt he and Young had similar personalities, the minister cheerfully acknowledges, "He's a lot nicer than I am."

The composition of the rest of the task force was also a testament to Young's astuteness; the group included eight Liberal members of the Commons, and Senator H. A. (Bud) Olson, a former Liberal cabinet minister. Although it crossed the country as "the Government Task Force on the Canadian National Railway System," it was really a committee of the Liberal caucus. "Young was very skillful on this," Tellier says. "He got away with appointing a task force of Liberals only. And nobody ever raised that. Amazing."

Independent though Nault was, CN had a subtle influence on the hearings. Its vice-president of government affairs, David Todd, a member of the old guard whom Tellier respected, actually wrote the terms of reference for the task force. Moreover, Sandra Wood, manager of government affairs for CN and previously a legislative assistant to four ministers of transport, served as its secretary. CN could hardly have had a better pipeline. Wood influenced decisions on who would address the task force, how much time each of the speakers could take and the order in which they appeared. Tellier was the first witness. He was also the last.

In mid-November, Tellier infuriated Young. These two headstrong men would one day speak highly of each other, but in the fall of 1994 relations between them were edgy.

Young was a freshman cabinet minister with limited experience in dealing with the federal bureaucracy. Tellier was an acknowledged master at getting what he wanted from bureaucrats. Young was notorious for the abuse he had hurled at Brian Mulroney's Tory government. Tellier owed his job to Mulroney and, for seven years, had worked closely with Tory cabinets. Young sometimes behaved as though he believed a boss couldn't be effective without being offensive. So did Tellier. Both were outspoken to a fault. Neither was burdened by false modesty. Neither saw patience as a virtue.

Torrance Wylie witnessed the tension that arose between them in 1994. "It was terrible," he says quietly, shaking his head. "Just terrible."

"The thing you had to remember, and the thing I kept reminding our colleagues," Ed Lumley explains, "was that this was the minister's deal. It was Mr. Young whose name would be on the document. It was Mr. Young who had his neck stuck out. And if anything went wrong, it was Mr. Young who'd incur the wrath of the Canadian public." In Tellier's zeal to promote the privatization, he occasionally forgot whose deal it was.

Before Young had announced the rejection of the CP offer, before the task force had started its tour, Young told Tellier, in Lumley's presence, that no one at CN should talk publicly about what the government might or should do. "I remember it well," Lumley says, "because Paul and I immediately phoned Michael [Sabia] to make sure he understood the minister's instructions. Even before this, Michael and I had been suggesting to Paul that the less said the better."

Young's instructions, alas, did not stop Tellier from making a speech to the Montreal Board of Trade in which he boldly declared, "Among all the options available, privatization is the best solution for CN, its employees and customers." He expressed his "profound conviction" that CN could become a company to make Canadians proud, and tossed out dollar figures that showed the railway might already be turning the corner towards profitability.

"Doug was very, *very* upset," Lumley says. "He was absolutely *smoking.* I mean, we were worried about Paul losing his job. I called him, and I said, 'Paul, buy the biggest cork you can find, and every time you feel like saying something in public, dip it into your favourite drink, and just suck on it as hard as you can. This is your friend calling, Paul. It's not your financial adviser, it's your friend.' "

He managed to restore peace and would do so again. "Ed Lumley in those days," Sabia says, "performed a crucial service. He very, very skillfully played the matchmaker [for Young and Tellier]. He had them out to little dinners. He built lines of communication. He planted seeds and watered them."

"Should you choose to commercialize CN," Tellier told the Liberal task force in mid-December, "we are ready to make a success of it. We are convinced we can."

He argued that privatizing CN would enable it to raise equity capital, thus freeing it from the endless borrowing that drove its debt sky-high. It would then grow stronger financially, and become more innovative. With the realities of the North American market-place governing its operations, he continued, CN would perform more efficiently than ever before. The privatization would enable management to forge better and more flexible partnerships with labour. All this would mean a major contribution to the prosperity of Canadian manufacturers and resource producers.

By then, however, a rift had opened on the committee. The last thing that Young, Tellier and CN's advisers wanted was a partial privatization of CN, but that's what three of the nine MPs promoted. In the disappointing Initial Public Offerings of Air Canada and Petro-Canada, the government had kept substantial chunks of the stock for itself, arousing a suspicion among potential investors that it would meddle in the affairs of the "privatized" companies.

Young wanted the government not only to sell 100 per cent of CN but, gigantic though the stock offering would be, to unload it all in one swoop. "If there's a deity in charge of IPOs," he said, "I pray to him every night that it's a one-shot affair."

Nault knew Young wanted the task force not just to recommend the sale of CN, holus bolus, but to recommend it unanimously. That way, doubters in cabinet could not say, "Look, there's no consensus even on our own caucus committee." Six members of the task force agreed, but the others insisted the government keep a stake in the corporation. Their motives varied. Ron MacDonald, for instance, member of Parliament for Dartmouth, Nova Scotia, hoped the government's partially owning CN would guarantee the eternal survival of the main line between central Canada and Halifax.

The debate continued for days. When the holdouts proposed they issue a minority report, Nault protested, "Come on, we're all Liberals here." Among his more influential task-force collaborators, during the conversion of the dissenters, was David Walker, MP for Winnipeg-North Centre, who had once taught him political science at the University of Manitoba. Walker was now parliamentary secretary to Young's most powerful cabinet ally, finance minister Paul Martin. The ubiquitous Ed Lumley also showed up at the hearings and, to allay MacDonald's fears, argued that short lines might end up giving Nova Scotia better service to central Canada than CN had ever provided.

Early in 1995, with no "nays" to sap the impact, the task force gave Young what he wanted. Its very first recommendation was "that the Minister of Transport commit to a process leading to the full commercialization of the Canadian National Railways as a coast-to-coast main-line operation." The committee also recommended the government offer CN employees "participation in the recommended commercialized operation."

Tellier would later speak glowingly of Nault's performance as the committee chairman, but when the recommendations first appeared, the third one struck him as insulting. It urged Young to consider not only appointing "an independent interim managing organization to oversee the transition" to privatization, but also engaging "experienced managers with commercial railway experience from outside of the CN corporate culture." Tellier angrily complained to Young that CN had been full of railroaders, and they had turned it into a disaster. Moreover, he had surrounded himself with railroaders, competent ones from both within and without CN. "There were a number of things in that report that were not very flattering to management, and Paul was pretty upset about that," CN's chairman David McLean says.

McLean was another strong-willed character in the privatization saga. A lawyer, businessman and real-estate tycoon from Vancouver, former chairman of the Canadian Chamber of Commerce and son of an Alberta train dispatcher who worked for CN for almost half a century, McLean says, "I've always loved the railway." As a staunch Liberal, he had known Prime Minister Chrétien for over thirty years. He had served as a CN director until the mid-1980s, when the Conservatives came to power. In August 1994, Chrétien put him back on the board, and four months later named him chairman. In both physique and self-confidence, this west-coast millionaire was a big man.

He had been chairman less than two months when Tellier and Young had their spat over the task force's recommendation number three. "It started out with the two of them really going at each other, and they were both right," McLean says. "I sort of sat in the middle as the referee. The task force wanted a trustee appointed and management to step aside, and this was just unrealistic. But Doug said, 'I'm only concerned about recommendation number one. All the other stuff is just Nault and those guys giving us their point of view.' I finally said, 'Paul, the minister's right. All that matters is that first recommendation, so let's not worry about the details.' And then we had a very good meeting for about two hours."

That single recommendation ("full commercialization" of the railway), the result of deliberations after hearings all across

Canada, helped Young gain support for CN's privatization from the Liberal caucus, and *that* helped him gain its approval in cabinet. As 1995 began, the task-force report nudged the government and CN close to the starting line of what Torrance Wylie called "the sprint." On February 27, 1995, while introducing his second budget to the Commons, Paul Martin would fire the starting pistol.

CHAPTER 7

Three Very *Strong* Personalities

Doug Young and his House of Commons allies like Robert Nault and David Walker had to sell certain Liberal MPs on the privatization of CN. It had not been in the famous Red Book of Liberal campaign vows. The creation of crown corporations was a part of Liberal culture; selling off the biggest of them all seemed an oddly Tory thing to do. Whether the survival of CN as a crown agency suited commercial realities, it still suited the ideology of many Liberal MPs. Moreover, some feared that in their constituencies, privatization would lead to the abandonment of rail lines, the shutting-down of shops and yards, and the destruction of jobs.

Bob Nault not only helped deliver the unanimous task-force recommendation Young wanted, but later promoted it in the Liberal caucus. "These things are sort of esoteric to people who don't understand them," Young says, "but you cannot get something through

Parliament simply because the prime minister and the minister responsible think it's important. You've got 293 other people . . . Nault was absolutely essential in networking through the Liberal caucus."

Ed Lumley, meanwhile, talked to the cabinet ministers he suspected were uncomfortable with the privatization. He argued that what made a Liberal a Liberal lay in the social programs that Grit governments had given Canadians, many of them the achievements of finance minister Paul Martin Jr.'s father. Trying to save what the late Paul Martin had created, his son was wrestling with "one of the toughest jobs in Canadian history." To succeed, he had to reduce the government's cash requirements and deficit, and ultimately Canada's debt. In this context, Lumley said, privatizing CN made so much sense it faced no powerful opposition in cabinet.

"The national dream of iron horses, steel rails and steam is dead," Young said publicly. "Today, Canadians see Medicare, Old Age Security, education and other social programs as the essential goals of government." In late January 1995, he revealed that the government planned a public share offering of CN, possibly even before the year was out.

Paul Tellier and CN chairman David McLean, meanwhile, went to London to pick the brains of British executives who had experienced major privatizations. They consulted top officers of British Steel, British Rail and PowerGen. McLean remembers a particularly fruitful meeting with "Steve Robson of Her Majesty's Treasury Board, who'd been involved in at least a dozen privatizations." The new chairman returned to Canada convinced that the government must go to world capital markets to privatize CN, and before doing that, must eliminate much of its debt. Among Young, Tellier, Michael Sabia and their advisers, a consensus was building on both points.

In mid-February, with Martin's budget speech not two weeks away—and all the privatization promoters chewing their nails over whether it would include their goal—another incident sabotaged relations between Tellier and Young.

"We had a meeting with Doug," McLean says, "and we were very concerned about leaks. We were saying to him, the minister, to be very careful who you're talking to, etc., etc. . . . And I think it was the very next day, Paul met with the editorial board of the *Globe and Mail*, and the whole thing ended up on page one [of the *Globe*'s Report on Business]."

Under "CN president takes hard line on union talks," the story said that if unions launched rotating strikes against CN in March, Tellier would lock them out and demand back-to-work legislation. It quoted him as saying, "Hopefully, the government will show some backbone and legislate them back to work in four or five days." He wanted Young "to set the guidelines of a contract" that would eliminate the current jobs-for-life guarantees for thousands of unionized employees. With respect to CP's having walked away from the merger talks the previous summer, Tellier predicted, "History will say they made a very great mistake." He told the *Globe* that, after more than a year of consultations with Nesbitt Burns and Morgan Stanley, he knew CN could be successfully privatized; he hoped to achieve the privatization as early as the coming summer, possibly through a $2-billion stock issue in the U.S.; the government would have to change its foreign-ownership legislation to sell CN to Americans; and CN's huge tracts of prime downtown land in Canadian cities might be used to pay off some of its $2.45-billion debt.

"I can tell you, the transport minister was not amused," McLean says. "Nor was the prime minister. I spent a lot of time on the telephone soothing over ruffled feelings, and assuring people this was a one-time error and would never happen again."

"Paul went to the *Globe* to defend himself," Lumley explains, "but in the process he let out some numbers. He assumed it was all off the record, which one must never assume—especially one who's been deputy minister to several prominent ministers and the clerk of the privy council."

Tellier's indiscretion angered not only Chrétien, but also Martin. Young was apoplectic. When the story appeared, he phoned Lumley and, as though the Nesbitt Burns vice-chairman shared responsibility for Tellier's utterances, snarled, "Are you guys stupid?" Lumley remembers warning Young that if he fired Tellier, "You can kiss your IPO good-bye, because he's doing a terrific job." If it weren't for Tellier's performance, he said, the government wouldn't even be thinking of privatizing CN.

Young did not fire Tellier. Their differences vanished in the hugeness, complexity and speed of the privatization effort. Under intense pressure, each grew thankful for the formidable abilities of the other.

On Wednesday, February 22, five days before budget night, James A. Runde, worldwide head of transportation coverage for Morgan Stanley, gave a graphic presentation to CN's top twenty executives about the suddenly dynamic railway industry south of the border, successful railway IPOs of recent years, why American railway shares had become glamour stocks and what CN should do to ensure the success of its own privatization. To get CN's leaders thinking hard about transforming the crown corporation into a real business and themselves into real business executives, Tellier had invited them to a retreat in the Laurentians in rural Quebec.

Another speaker was Claude Taylor who, as head of Air Canada, had already endured a major privatization. "Looking back," Tellier asked, "what would you have done differently?" Taylor replied that Air Canada had seriously underestimated the importance of changing its corporate culture. The culture of a government-coddled crown agency could never suit a private outfit fighting hot competition. Even as Taylor spoke, CN's culture was changing. His audience seemed eager to show the world it could run a real railway.

Wes Kelley was in the crowd. A public relations man, he had joined CN thirty-four years before and had been bouncing from city to city on behalf of various CN enterprises ever since. As the privatization effort loomed, Torrance Wylie convinced Tellier it would require a public relations professional who knew CN from stem to gudgeon. No one filled the bill better than Kelley. He was happy where he was, in Edmonton, but in January 1995, "Paul Tellier showed up in my office, a glass of orange juice in hand, to discuss the situation."

On Wednesday, February 22, Kelley was listening to Runde in the Laurentians. On Friday, back in Edmonton, he got orders from Tellier to report to CN headquarters by Sunday night because Paul Martin would announce the privatization of CN in his budget on Monday. Kelley reached Montreal just in time. Not stopping even to park his luggage at a hotel, he went straight to a meeting at CN and then performed his first job as vice-president, public affairs and advertising. He supervised the writing of a press release about CN's reaction to the budget announcement.

"Our view is straightforward," Martin told the Commons the next day. If government doesn't *need* to run something, it *shouldn't*. And in the future, it *won't* . . . Today, we are announcing that the Minister of Transport will initiate steps this year to sell CN."

"From then on," Sabia recalls, "we just went like a bat out of hell to get this thing done."

"We worked very hard at getting it into the budget," says David Todd, CN's vice-president, government affairs, Ottawa. "We did a lot of lobbying. And, of course, the finance department, the whole government, is so intensely secretive just before the budget date, we couldn't find out what was going on."

"We didn't know when it would be announced," Tellier remembers, "but Mr. Young just said, 'Leave it to me.' And he did persuade the minister of finance to put it in the budget speech. Of course, he had the full support of the prime minister—otherwise this wouldn't have taken place—but Mr. Young was just superb in managing this around the cabinet table. Just superb."

How, exactly, did Young induce Martin to include the privatization in the budget? "You can't control people on things like that," Young says. "They either think it's the right thing to do, or they don't. And Paul Martin is too capable a fellow to manipulate. We have an extremely good relationship. Getting it in there, of course, really fast-tracked the legislative process."

"Doug Young's smartest play, by far, and this was done in conjunction with Paul Martin," Torrance Wylie explains, "was to communicate the decision in the budget. Once the privatization was in the budget, the way this government operates, it was formally on the agenda. You don't have to execute against your policy announcements. You do have to execute against your budget statements, and that's why this was extremely important. The budget was the green light. From that day on, the privatization was ours to screw up, but otherwise it was going to happen."

Everyone was expecting strikes at CN and CP in March, as well as the possibility of the back-to-work legislation Tellier had so rashly urged in the *Globe*—and binding arbitration. The budget declaration warned the unions that the ancient negotiating rituals, at least at CN, were about to change. "So it was very astute not to let that [privatization] decision hang out there till the end," Wylie continues, "and to bring it forward in the budget."

Like Young, Paul Martin was a lawyer who had turned himself into a millionaire businessman. His late father, whom he had idolized, served in the cabinets of four Liberal prime ministers and in Windsor, Ontario, won no fewer than ten federal elections. The younger Martin, however, didn't run for public office until he was fifty. In 1981, after working for Power Corporation in Montreal for a dozen years, he pulled off a leveraged buyout of the corporation's Canada Steamship Lines (CSL). To do so, he bet his farm, a big spread in the Eastern Townships, enlisted a partner to help pay the $195-million price, and with interest rates at an all-time high, borrowed heavily. With him at the helm, however, CSL sailed into profitability. He was a gambler, a bit of a showman.

As finance minister, Martin's bluntness horrified some bureaucrats. He dismissed their jargon-ridden briefing papers as "crap" and demanded concise advice in plain English. At one memorable meeting, he called tax officials "you stupid bastards." His executive assistant, Terrie O'Leary, has said, "He believes in tension. He sees it in a positive light." Among bureaucrats with sufficiently thick skins to survive them, his tirades were "the Beatings." The Beatings became both an inside joke and a bond, like college initiations. Despite his outbursts, Martin engendered extraordinary loyalty among his officials. He could be witty, charming, thoughtful, courteous and as genial as he was abusive. He had the air of a statesman. By bureaucratic standards, however, he was a man in a very big hurry.

"The bureaucracy is very process-oriented and I'm not," he said in *Double Vision: The Inside Story of the Liberals in Power*, by Edward Greenspon and Anthony Wilson-Smith. "Nobody who has been in business *is*. I basically want to get a job done. I don't give a damn about the process. For the bureaucracy, what's interesting is that as long as the process is working, everybody is happy. The thing can go on for years. We don't *have* years."

Thus, Martin, Tellier and Young had something in common other than volcanic tempers. The transport minister and the CN boss, that convert from the ways of the bureaucracy to the creed of the corporate world, also believed with a vengeance in getting a job done while not giving a damn about the process.

"There are three *very* strong personalities in the story," says W. David Wilson, president of ScotiaMcLeod. "Doug Young absolutely *drove* the thing. He doesn't give a shit about any impediment. He just drives right over it. And at those pivotal moments when what was needed was common sense, Paul Martin was there. He brought wisdom to the table and a steady, even, balanced hand. When Young started to scream and try to pick fights, Martin stepped in. He let Young take the limelight, but stayed close enough to keep everything sensible."(A year after the privatization, the *Globe and Mail* would rank Martin as Canada's best cabinet minister, with Young a close second, despite his managing "to needlessly irritate and antagonize virtually everyone, critic and comrade.")

"The third personality was Paul Tellier," Wilson continues. "He found this sleepy old pig [CN], full of fat, bad management and debt, and decided to do something about it. And with Sabia's help, he did."

Among departments trying to help finance minister Martin slash government spending, *Double Vision* reported, "The prize pupil was Transport [under Young], which had zoomed well ahead of the pack in redefining its mission and shedding costs." The finance department had controlled previous privatizations, yet Martin assigned CN's not to his own bureaucrats but to Transport Canada. Never before had "a line minister" like Young handled a major privatization file.

"There were some objections to this, but it was very much my decision," Martin says, "and it was totally the result of my confidence in Doug Young. I knew he'd get on with it and do it expeditiously and capably. I spent my whole life in business. If you've got someone who can do a job, you give it to him and let him carry the ball."

"Paul Martin and the people at finance were absolutely superb," Young acknowledges. "No line minister had ever done a privatization, so for them to have enough of a comfort level to sort of stand back, and say, 'You can go ahead and do this,' was remarkable in its own right."

Senior bureaucrats in the finance department later played an important role in setting the price CN fetched, but in early 1995, despite Young's memory, their comfort level was not high enough to prevent them fretting about the number of CN and transport department officials involved in the biggest transaction in Canadian government history. "They were chomping at the bit," Lumley says. "They knew this discussion was going on, and yet they weren't involved. I kept saying to them, 'Trust me, the way CN and Transport Canada are carrying out this work, it's as if you people were in there yourselves. You'll still get a ton of work, but at least you won't have to start from scratch.' "

Young made sure that, whenever senior Transport Canada officials met to discuss important privatization matters, they asked bureaucrats from finance to join them. "We were totally transparent," he says.

What astonished Tellier, who had spent so much of his life watching cabinet ministers shepherd legislation through Parliament, was the speed of Young's performance. On July 13, just 136 days after the budget speech, Bill C-89, the CN Commercialization Act, received Royal Assent and became law. "I had never seen a decision announced and a bill introduced and passed so quickly," Tellier marvels. "I mean, it's a record."

Young says the justice department officials who drafted the legislation, his parliamentary secretary, Joe Fontana, MP for London East, and Solicitor General Herbert Gray, house leader for the Liberals, all helped speed the passage of Bill C-89. "It was extremely important to keep it moving quickly," Young explains. "If you leave anything hanging out there too long, even if it's the best deal in the world, it'll come apart."

The tight schedule became an ally. "Tellier used it to drive the company, Young and Martin used it to drive decisions in Ottawa, and well-meaning bureaucrats never had the time to nitpick," says former well-meaning bureaucrat Michael Sabia. Back in the fall of 1994, Sabia also remembers, "We were saying, 'Yeah, wouldn't it be great to proceed with privatization, but Doug Young was saying, 'Yeah, wouldn't it be great to proceed with privatization *now*." Yankee ballplayer Reggie Jackson once called himself "the straw that stirred the drink in New York City." Sabia calls Young "the straw that stirred the drink in the privatization of CN." Wylie calls him "the man of the hour."

"I have never seen a minister manage a file as effectively and rapidly as Mr. Young did," Tellier says. "He was the champion. Without Doug Young, Canadian National would not have been privatized. This is really his personal achievement."

Head to Head with the Unions

The train is set to depart, but the conductor checks the refrigerator in the locomotive cab and discovers it doesn't contain a bottle of water. He therefore rules the train cannot leave the station. And that, Paul Tellier says, was but one example of the power unions had to sabotage railway efficiency. Here's another. A mechanic is disconnecting an electric motor. He can easily handle the job himself but, if it takes him more than a certain number of minutes, he must down tools and call in an electrician. The electrician "owns" the work. "Under existing contracts," *Maclean's* reported in 1994, "a diesel mechanic is not allowed to change a locomotive's headlight." With identical skills, some tradesmen could work only on cars, and others only on locomotives.

"In our repair shops, we had a myriad of crafts, all with ownership over their work," says Jack McBain, senior vice-president, operations.

The employees included carmen, blacksmiths, boilermakers, electricians, machinists, sheet-metal workers, millworkers, pipefitters and labourers. Tellier aimed to eliminate "trade barriers in the shop" and have CN train "highly skilled composite employees" who would be equally familiar with computers and locomotives.

Another obstacle on the road towards efficiency lay in crew schedules that made no competitive sense at all. A train bound from Sarnia to Halifax, with petrochemicals for export, dropped off its first crew in Toronto, and a second one climbed aboard. This happened again in Belleville, Montreal, Charny, Edmundston and Moncton. Six changes.

As if job ownership and excessive crew changes weren't enough to hamstring CN operations, the corporation had to abide by the wasteful "dual basis of pay" for engineers and conductors. As old as the century, the system paid wages according to the hours an employee had worked, _or_ the miles he or she had travelled—whichever produced the fatter pay packet. For a train that went 250 miles in ten hours, the arrangement paid the crew not just for those ten hours, but for two-and-a-half days.

"The system has been made even more complex and costly through the negotiation of so-called arbitrary payments, for time not worked," Donald C. Fraleigh, a former CN labour negotiator, wrote in a 1994 report to Transport Canada. CN estimated that "current non-productive payments associated with this system of pay cost $79 million per annum." Collective agreements also forced CN to keep unnecessary crew aboard many trains, costing a further $18 million per year.

CN's locomotive engineers earned $36 per hour—more than twice as much as most truck drivers. Indeed, the average wage in Canadian railways was 49 percent higher than in trucking. But the real labour-cost killer was job security. It crippled CN's ability to shrink its payroll by closing plants, shedding network or exploiting advanced technology. Employment security was an entitlement among thousands of union members who had been with CN for eight years or more. If CN laid them off, they could stay home, drawing full wages and benefits right up until their retirement pensions kicked in. Nor did they have to accept jobs that CN offered in other parts of Canada.

"It was extremely hard for us to have to hire and train people, mostly in western Canada," Tellier says, "and at the same time, to have people on employment security, without useful work to do, in eastern Canada."

Of the 11,000 jobs Tellier swore CN would abolish by the end of 1995, Fraleigh's report explained, 1,800 were held by workers with employment security—"with an average annual cost, over ten years, of $37 million per year." CP was in a similar fix. Was it any wonder that labour productivity on Canadian railways hovered at about 60 per cent of that of major American lines?

It was compliant governments and gullible railway managements, Michael Sabia says, that enabled the unions to land such extravagant settlements. The unions would start negotiations by making outrageous demands. If the railway didn't promptly roll over and give them what they wanted, they called "a fairly painless and polite sort of strike." They knew what would happen next. Politicians would pass back-to-work legislation, saying, "Well, we won't give them everything they're asking, only half."

"If the starting point is the sun, the moon and the stars," Sabia continues, "and you get 50 per cent, that's a pretty good deal. And if that happens four or five times, we end up with these completely nonsensical labour agreements."

But it wasn't politicians who in 1985 gave the unions employment security. "That wasn't government," Sabia insists. "It was management. Let's just speak about CN. It was CN management who gave the unions the first lifetime employment security. Their justification was, 'Oh, we'll never have to downsize again, so we'll just hand them the sleeves out of our best clothes.' I mean, Christ, these people needed their heads examined!"

Not only the "commercialization" reference in the budget, but also Tellier's aggressive attitude towards the unions warned them that the old negotiating games were gone forever. Edward G. Abbot of the Canadian Railway Labour Association (CRLA) attacked Tellier's "cryptic and mysterious" behaviour and "three-pronged strategy" of labour relations: "One day, Mr. Tellier meets with the union general chairmen, asking for their cooperation; the next day he makes a speech castigating provisions of the unions' collective agreements; another day, he holds a press conference advising that he would lay off 10,000 employees."

Abbot believed that Tellier, as far back as 1993, had a secret plan to precipitate a rail strike and thereby pressure government to pass laws to solve CN's labour problems. "Mr. Tellier is either the most Machiavellian individual in Canada," Abbot said, "or the most hard-working, honest chief executive officer in North America. Only time will answer this question."

"If Tellier was a hawk on the labour issue," says one CN vice-president, "and Tellier *was* a hawk on this thing, then Young was a screaming eagle."

With the full support of the screaming eagle, both CN and CP took a hard line in the labour negotiations of early 1995. "Neither of us was willing to simply tinker with the existing collective agreements," Sabia says. "We were determined to secure the flexibility we required to build modern, efficient railways."

Three weeks after the budget announcement, a national rail strike was costing CN $9.5 million a day, and the Canadian Manufacturers Association claimed the damage to the Canadian economy would soon reach $3 billion. The strike lasted eight days. At the end of March, Parliament passed back-to-work legislation. The fine hand of Tellier colleague Alphonse Giard, CN's vice-president, law, had something to do with it. Giard had prepared material for the legislation, which Young had passed along to human resources development minister Lloyd Axworthy. The bill included the imposition of binding arbitration on the railways and unions, and a unique instruction to the arbitration commissions. No previous back-to-work legislation had ever demanded this: "Each commission shall be guided by the need for terms and conditions of employment that are *consistent with the economic viability and competitiveness of a coast-to-coast rail system in both the short and the long term . . .*" (emphasis added).

Not only Paul Martin and Doug Young, but other cabinet ministers deserve credit for CN's historic privatization. Ed Lumley says it was Axworthy, for instance, who accepted the responsibility for inserting in the labour legislation the reference to viability and competitiveness, "and if that hadn't happened, this [the privatization] wouldn't have happened."

To Abbot of the CRLA, this provision gave credence to "the Bloc Québécois allegations that the hidden agenda of minister Young and CN Rail CEO Paul Tellier is to use the legislation to gut the railway unions' collective agreements by arbitration." To Young, however, the need for the arbitration commissions to consider the survival and competitiveness of Canada's rail system was as obvious as the orange snout of a CN locomotive.

"When I suggested this was going to be in [the legislation]," Young says, "all hell broke loose because it was felt in some quarters that it would prejudice us. It had never been done before, but I thought it was the most practical thing. As a matter of fact, I was appalled that anyone would suggest economic viability should *not* be in."

In mid-July, the chairman of the arbitration commissions, Judge George Adams of the Ontario court general division, released rulings that pleased the railways and distressed the unions. He maintained employment security, but watered it down. No workers hired after January 1, 1994, would receive it. Benefits would no longer last until retirement age, but for just six years, and anyone collecting them would have to be ready to move to a railway job anywhere in the country.

Even before the commissions completed their reports, CN reached agreements with 7,800 unionized employees. Some of the deals enabled the railway to reduce the crafts in maintenance operations from seven to three; cut the transit time between Toronto and Vancouver by six hours; eliminate nine stops for crew changes between Halifax and Vancouver; and install microwave ovens in locomotives to enable crews to eat without stopping their trains. One agreement, Canada News-Wire reported, "provides CN with some of the best operational work rules of any railway in North America—for crews working up to 12 hours on extended runs."

The unions abhorred the commissions' rulings. Referring to three union representatives who had participated in the arbitration process, Gary Fane of the Canadian Auto Workers (CAW) snarled, "Not all unions or union leaders are created equal. Some serve the employers first and the workers second. CP Rail and CN Rail should be eternally thankful to the three Amigos, well known as the three weak siblings."

"We're damn mad," said Bob Chernecki, another CAW spokesman. Like other union executives, however, he felt the enforced settlement "could have been a hell of a lot worse."

The agreements and rulings of the spring of 1995 helped CN and CP reduce labour costs; offer more reliable, timely and flexible service; and survive the competition from American lines that, with respect to labour productivity, had long been clobbering them. Later, Gordon Lackenbauer, deputy chairman of Nesbitt Burns, remembered the arbitrated settlement as "absolutely critical" to the privatization. When Young insisted the arbitrators use the economic viability of the railways as a guideline, the banker added, "He loaded the dice."

"Because," said Lackenbauer's associate Evan Siddall, "the dice *had* to be loaded."

This Time, They'd Do It Right

P aul Tellier and Michael Sabia not only knew how the federal bureaucracy worked, but during their civil-service careers had dealt with the very officials the government assigned to CN's privatization. These included David Dodge, deputy minister of finance; Nick Mulder, deputy minister of transport; and Moya Green, transport's assistant deputy minister, policy.

A handful of Transport Canada staff, Doug Young says, responded magnificently to the privatization challenges. Led by Moya Green, they "represented my interests, the interests of the people of Canada, face-to-face with institutional giants like Goldman, Sachs and Nesbitt Burns, and boy, I had every confidence we wouldn't come out on the short end of the stick. And we didn't."

Having often worked together in the public service, Sabia and

Green enjoyed what Sabia called "a pre-established rapport." When a privatization problem arose, they often solved it by phone before the matter became destructive. Aware that finance officials distrusted Transport Canada's control over the privatization process, Green set up an interdepartmental committee to keep them fully informed. CN's closeness to the bankers aroused doubts in finance about their commitment to maximizing the government's take, but Green helped allay these worries.

"She was a conduit between us and government, and an important conduit within government," Sabia says. "She wasn't turf-conscious, nor paranoid about our relationship with the banks. I was on the phone with her three or four times a week, and sometimes anywhere from five to ten times a day."

Long known to both Tellier and Sabia, David Dodge was a tall, tweedy, pipe-smoking ex-professor. According to the authors of _Double Vision_, he "still looked more the academic than the Ottawa power-broker." Ed Lumley had known Dodge since his own years in Ottawa as an MP and cabinet minister. About his part in the privatization, Paul Martin said, "David was a _very_ constructive force throughout the whole thing."

Regarding Tellier's role in the privatization, Young begins, "You've got to give the devil his due." Tellier knew where the bureaucratic roadblocks and bottlenecks would be. "The process, internally, is time-consuming," Young explains. "You have to jump through a lot of hoops. And we were also doing the National Transportation Act, because the success of the share offering would be very dependent on how investors saw the future of railroads in Canada. So we were on two tracks at the same time.

"We had to deal with the debt, the disposition of CN's non-rail assets, and the makeup of a consortium to handle the issue domestically and internationally. We had to fight over its [the consortium's] structure, who would lead it, how to decide on pricing, whether or not this would be a one-shot affair and all that. And because of Tellier's unique experience, having been with the Privy

Council Office and then on the business side of it at CN, he understood the obstacles."

It was part of Tellier's management style to encourage people
whose judgement he respected to reach their own conclusions—and
express them frankly. He therefore had his own brain trust, which
met every Tuesday afternoon in the CN boardroom. The membership varied, but as the privatization effort roared towards the summer of 1995, the regulars included Sabia; Lumley, Wes Kelley and
Torrance Wylie; Jeff Ward of A. T. Kearney; CN's Canadian lawyer,
Jean-Pierre Ouellet of Stikeman Elliott, Montreal; CN's American
lawyer, Winthrop B. Conrad Jr. of Davis Polk & Wardwell, New
York; and executives from the three "global coordinators" for the
privatization: Goldman, Sachs & Co., Nesbitt Burns Inc., and
ScotiaMcLeod Inc.

"These weren't worker bees," Winthrop Conrad recalls. "They
were senior people strategizing on issues. We discussed the big pic-
ture. We set agendas and schedules for legislative, political, marketing, restructuring and regulatory issues, and debt reduction. We
talked about different things at each meeting. But that's just the
Tuesday afternoon meetings. There were a lot more than that."

"Much of the credit [for the success of the privatization] should
go to a first-class team of outside advisers," Sabia says. "They
fought all the time. But the wild and raucous sessions we had—the
competitive dynamic among them that we wanted from the start—
was a boon to the whole process."

Among the outside advisers whose experience and dedication
Sabia heavily relied on was Jeff Ward. During the merger talks with
CP, the A. T. Kearney consultant had learned so much about CN
that, in Sabia's words, he proved "absolutely indispensable in helping us arrange all the elements of this turnaround and frame the
basic story for the privatization."

Many of the Canadian leaders of the privatization were millionaire
Liberals, businessmen and old friends. Chairman David McLean

had known the prime minister for more than thirty years. Torrance Wylie, who had served as senior political adviser to prime ministers Lester Pearson and Pierre Trudeau, had known Tellier for just as long.

When Tellier joined CN, he turned to Wylie, then the executive vice-president of Imasco Ltd., for advice on how to run a huge corporation. Imasco, a tobacco, financial services, fast food, drugstores and real-estate development giant, has 57,000 employees. Wylie would later become chairman of Government Policy Consultants (GPC), Ottawa, which counted both CN and Imasco among its clients. Paul Martin had once been a director of Imasco. In the spring of 1995, Young appointed Purdy Crawford, the highly respected chairman of Imasco, to CN's board.

"I already knew Paul Tellier well," Crawford says, "through his involvement with government." Crawford had persuaded Tellier to succeed him as a co-head of the United Way in Montreal. When Cedric Ritchie, former chairman of the Bank of Nova Scotia, joined the CN board, he and Tellier were no strangers to each other, either. "I knew Paul from his days in Ottawa," Ritchie says, "plus the fact that he has a ski chalet close to me up at Sainte-Adèle."

Gordon Lackenbauer, deputy chairman of Nesbitt Burns, one of the Canadian global coordinators, and David Wilson, president of the other, ScotiaMcLeod, were friends with such respect for each other that, despite the fierce pressures of the privatization effort, relations between their rival firms remained harmonious. "I had known Gordon Lackenbauer a long time," Paul Martin says, "and I knew David Wilson."

Ed Lumley, Nesbitt Burns's vice-chairman, had known Martin since their teenage years in Windsor, Ontario, and having held five cabinet posts, knew myriad senior bureaucrats and Liberals in high places. As a director of Air Canada, he knew chairman Claude Taylor, a veteran of the airline's privatization.

"Every project like this has days when it's on the floor and seems headed for the basement and a deep, dark hole that it'll never come out of," Wylie says. "Well, we had those days, and Ed Lumley was the glue that kept this thing going through some very tense periods. One of the imperatives was to trust the investment bankers, the government and the corporation. These had to all come together, and Ed was at the centre of those trust relationships from start to finish. When things got dicey, he put it all back together."

If there was one conviction the politicians, bureaucrats, bankers and CN executives all shared, it was that this privatization—unlike those of Air Canada and Petro-Canada—had to be done right. It was past time Canada showed the world it could sell a major crown corporation without bungling.

Limiting foreign ownership to 25 per cent, the government began to sell chunks of Air Canada in 1988. Tens of thousands of buyers snapped up shares at $8, but by the spring of 1995, the price had sunk to $6. On March 29, in what was then one of the biggest single public offerings in Canadian business history, Air Canada raised $500 million. The deal, however, was a flop. "The sudden flood of new shares choked the market and quickly knocked more than a dollar off the $7.50 value of Air Canada's shares," *Maclean's* reported. "That enraged dozens of powerful pension and mutual fund managers whose firms already owned sizable positions in Air Canada." By one estimate, the underwriting syndicate for the offering immediately dropped $12 million. The lead underwriter was none other than CN banker Nesbitt Burns, which managed to unload its own piece of the deal without a loss.

The story of Petro-Canada, for which Tellier had served as a board member, was less grim, yet still far from satisfying. The government sold 30 per cent of the company to the public in 1991 at $13 a share. Four years later, the price was around $12. Petro-Canada was performing well, but Ottawa's retaining 70 per cent of the shares discouraged investors and depressed the share price. "Some shareholders who forked over savings for chunks of Petro-Canada and Air Canada," wrote Vic Parsons of Canadian Press, "may wish they had spent their money on trips to Las Vegas."

The compulsion to ensure success begat unprecedented decisions. "The first bit of boldness, and indeed, 'recklessness' is almost certainly the better word," Sabia remembers, "was to privatize 100 per cent of CN when most commentators thought it couldn't be done. The risk-averse strategy you'd have expected from CN and the government would have been to sell 20 per cent, declare victory and decide what to do next. But neither wanted the substantial government overhangs in the market that had plagued Air Canada and Petro-Canada."

Would it be possible to sell more than $2 billion in CN shares at one crack in a market as small as Canada's? Young didn't think so. "It would be naive to think the Canadian market can take it all up," he said publicly in May 1995. As far back as budget time, he and other key privatizers had decided the deal simply had to be international.

If potential investors in Canada thought about CN at all, they envisaged a sinkhole under the supervision of blundering bureaucrats who couldn't run a mom-and-pop store. Canadian investors were not only largely contemptuous of CN, but largely ignorant of the booming railway industry in the U.S. By arousing interest in CN among railway sophisticates in the American investment community, the privatization strategists hoped to lure Canadians into investing in the IPO. American investors generally hated buying into partnerships with government.

Prodded by Young, the cabinet therefore followed its first bold decision with an even bolder one. It ruled that no shareholder could own more than 15 per cent of the stock, but aside from that, imposed no restrictions on foreign ownership. This was a first in the history of privatizing major crown corporations in Canada.

"Doug Young was very supportive of this," Chairman McLean says, "but I also had some private meetings with the prime minister to discuss it. He had difficulty with it because it was a big change in policy for him. But he listened very carefully. I told him we had been to the United Kingdom and seen a lot of the U.K. corporations, and one of the things that struck me was that the reason they were successful in doing these $3- or $4-billion deals was that they had access to world capital markets. They were in London, and there were no restrictions on foreign ownership.

"So the prime minister said to me, 'Do you think that in order to get the best price for the government, we're going to have to do something?' And I said, 'Absolutely.' So my recommendation to him was that we eliminate all foreign ownership restrictions—which I think was a pretty major departure from where the government had been coming from—but that there be a restriction on the number of shares [that any corporation could hold] . . . So somebody like Canadian Pacific or Union Pacific couldn't come in and buy control of CN."

The government's decision, Sabia says, "represented an enormous leap of faith. The story of Canadian companies going global was littered with failures . . . And there we were, CN, that well-known business giant, reaching for the moon. This was going to be Canada's first truly global deal."

Past ownership restrictions had signalled that the government tolerated yet did not welcome foreign investors. "This time we put out the welcome mat," Sabia says, "and to a lot of people's surprise, the world came calling." The welcome included decisions to list the shares not just in Canada but also on the New York Stock Exchange, and to choose an international banker, Goldman, Sachs, as one of the IPO's global coordinators. Again, these decisions were Canadian privatization firsts.

Not only Prime Minister Chrétien, but others in the cabinet and Liberal caucus were initially uncomfortable about the absence of foreign ownership restrictions. Indeed, the idea troubled Paul Martin for a while. But since Canadian law regulated CN and forced it to keep its headquarters in Montreal, since the bulk of CN's operations were in Canada, and since the 15 per cent restriction barred a takeover by a single foreign owner, he concluded further protection wasn't necessary.

Moreover, Martin explains, growing institutions require growing capital, much of which comes from international markets. "You don't want to stop the company's growth," Martin says, "and how do you marry this desire to keep a corporation Canadian and the need to bring in foreign capital? Nobody doubts that IBM is an American company [though its shareholders are around the world]. Sony is a Japanese company. You've got to marry those two things regardless of the share ownership."

Another reason for encouraging American investment lay in Tellier's conviction that CN had to quit thinking of itself as a Canadian operation and transform itself into the best freight railroad in North America. North-south trade was burgeoning. U.S. railways were swallowing one another to create ever bigger and more efficient lines. To survive, much less conquer, CN had to leap with both feet into this dynamic and ruthlessly competitive scene. It had to be a serious contender. It needed owners who knew all about the rival contenders, transportation economics and potential alliances in the continental struggle for railway supremacy.

In Canada, where CP Rail was part of a conglomerate, no pure railway traded on stock markets. Few investment banks boasted rail analysts, and few investors knew anything at all about railways. It would have surprised most Canadian money managers to hear that Americans had put twice as much money into rail stocks as airline stocks. Americans had invested tens of billions in freight railways, and at the big Manhattan banks railway analysis was a profession. To compete in North America, Tellier knew, CN needed railway-smart investors to ride herd on its operations. Such investors were almost all Americans.

Tellier wanted CN to compete in the railway big league south of the border for much the same reason that Wayne Gretzky wanted to play hockey in New York. "I really believe," Gretzky said, "that the kind of pressure New York puts on you makes you a better player."

In past privatizations, the government and the corporation on the block each had its own team of financial advisers. But the interests of the seller (the government), whose advisers pushed for the highest price possible, often conflicted with those of the corporation. A tug-of-war between the two teams, Tellier explains, could damage any privatization attempt. "Air Canada comes to mind," he says, "and Petro-Canada, in spades." Both IPOs, experts later decided, were overmanaged and overpriced. Investors lost interest.

With two sets of financial advisers, Wylie adds, "you're getting into a negotiation with your shareholder. Over *everything*. So you're no longer focused on how-do-I-get-this-thing-out-the-door-and-sold."

Both CN and the government wanted the biggest business transaction in the history of Canada to be a smash hit. Good for the government, they believed, good for the company. Good for the company, good for the government.

"There was no cleavage of interest," Sabia says. "But if you brought in another adviser for the government, then just the natural forces would dictate that that adviser would find things to criticize and change, and draw out a conflict between the government and us. That's how they make their money. That's how they show the client it makes sense to put the price higher, because if everything was amity and love the government would go, 'Well, why are you guys here? You're not telling us any different from what these other bankers are saying, and we hired you. Tell us something different.' "

Young, for his part, had no confidence in any investment bank that preferred a management fee to a share of the action: "If they felt the best deal in town was to get X number of bucks to give me a price, it didn't sound like they were very excited about the potential for the success of this issue. Why the hell would I want their advice?" He trusted the bureaucrats in the finance and transport departments, not only because they were capable, but because they had nobody's interest at heart except the Canadian taxpayers'. "You weren't going to get any better unfiltered advice," Young says. "They'd be making the same bucks the day after the issue, as the day before."

Gordon Lackenbauer of Nesbitt Burns said that, with respect to

Air Canada and Petro-Canada, the two-team system had proved costly and unsatisfactory. Having just one team might appear to invite a conflict of interest, but in reality the CN consortium had too much at stake—the reputation of its members—to have let down either the seller or the corporation. Young's perspective was a bit different. He would not have risked sharing just one set of financial advisers if they'd all come from the same bank, but the CN consortium, composed of three institutions, had "a healthy tension." In other words, "Before they screwed me, they had to screw one another. It was going to be a tough call."

Wylie calls the decision to rely for financial advice solely on the underwriting consortium "another triumph of Ed Lumley." It would not seem important to casual followers of the privatization saga, but to Wylie, "That's the reason this whole thing happened. *That's how you could have a sprint*. Ed Lumley did that."

Overleaf: In the fall of 1995, with the Initial Public Offering of CN shares looming, the railway ordered 105 new 4,300-horsepower locomotives from the diesel division of General Motors of Canada. It was the biggest locomotive order in CN's history. The corporation planned to buy around 300 more over the next fifteen years.

Among freight railways of North America, CN has one of the gentlest grades through the great western mountains to the Pacific coast.

Right: In 1992, Paul Tellier, Canada's top civil servant, was named president and chief executive officer of debt-ridden, crown-owned CN by Prime Minister Brian Mulroney. Industry experts predicted this "political appointment" of a bureaucrat with no railway experience would prove disastrous. In 1996, Tellier led the newly privatized CN to its best year in more than seven decades.

Top: Friction between strong-willed Minister of Transport Doug Young and strong-willed CN President Paul Tellier threatened to derail the privatization effort. Eventually, each learned that the other's talent, drive and pushiness were essential to the success of the biggest Initial Public Offering in Canadian history. PHOTO: CANADIAN PRESS

Bottom: Late in the winter of 1993, Michael Sabia was persuaded by Paul Tellier to quit his job as deputy secretary to the federal cabinet and join CN as senior vice-president, corporate development (later chief financial officer). Sabia, an Ottawa colleague says, has "an incredibly well-directed, strategic mind."

Top: After months of talks about merging CP's and CN's unprofitable eastern networks and plants into a new, joint railway, Barry Scott (*left*), chief executive officer of CP Rail System, broke off the negotiations and proposed that CP buy CN's eastern operations. That was in July, 1994. The government rejected the deal, and by autumn Tellier (*right*) and his staff were preparing the case for CN's privatization. PHOTO: CANADIAN PRESS

Bottom: David McLean of Vancouver was appointed CN chairman by Prime Minister Jean Chrétien in December 1994. McLean visited London, England, in early 1995, consulted executives of privatized British corporations and returned home convinced there should be no limit on foreign ownership of CN.

Top: Minister of Finance Paul Martin Jr. (*right*) with Prime Minister Jean Chrétien (*front left*) and Liberal House Leader Herb Gray (*front centre*). Martin declared in his budget speech of February 27, 1995, "Today, we are announcing that the Minister of Transport will initiate steps this year to sell CN." Just nine months later, the deed was done. PHOTO: J. M. CARISSE

Left: Of the CN veterans who survived Paul Tellier's dismissal of executives, none blossomed more creatively in the new atmosphere of urgency than Jack T. McBain, senior vice-president, operations. McBain played a starring role in the international road show to persuade money managers to buy CN shares.

Right: As vice-president, information systems and accounting, Ronan D. McGrath coordinated the elimination of thousands of jobs. The work, he said, was "the toughest possible. The choices were stark, but it had to be done."

Top left: Gerald K. Davies, a marketing pro who had worked for two major American railways, arrived at CN as senior vice-president, marketing, in late 1993. His most formidable challenge was to teach CN's poorly focused marketing staff to serve shippers as well as, or better than, the most efficient U.S. railways.

Top right: Claude Mongeau, vice-president, strategic and financial planning, worked closely with Michael Sabia. Shortly before the IPO, at least two dozen auditors, lawyers, bureaucrats, bankers, consultants and CN executives attended the privatization meetings. "It was like bringing home some huge boat," says Mongeau.

Bottom left: At the height of the privatization drive, says Wes Kelley, CN's vice-president, public affairs and advertising, "Just about everyone around here was putting in fifteen-hour days. We joked about it a lot. We'd say, 'Let's go down to the lobby and count the body bags.' "

Bottom right: In August 1995, just three months before the IPO, James M. Foote joined CN as vice-president, investor relations. Few people better knew the bankers who specialized in railroad deals, the railway analysts at brokerage houses and the institutional investors in U.S. lines.

To impress potential investors, the government abandoned the custom of naming political hacks and bagmen to the CN Board of Directors, and sought individuals with the best possible business credentials. CN soon boasted one of the most impressive boards in Canada. The directors were (*standing, left to right*) Jean Forest, Edward Neufeld, Denis Losier, Maureen Kempston Darkes, Raymond Cyr, Cedric Ritchie, Purdy Crawford, Robert Pace, Richard Kroft, and (*seated*) Paul Tellier and David McLean.

Top: With intermodal terminals at the best Canadian harbour on the Pacific, Vancouver (*pictured here*), and the best on the Atlantic, Halifax, CN feeds freight to North America from both coasts. It is the continent's only truly transcontinental railway.

Left: Jean-Pierre Ouellet of Stikeman Elliott, Canadian legal counsel to CN during the privatization campaign, later joined the corporation as its chief legal officer and corporate secretary.

Right: Jeff Ward of A. T. Kearney Inc., Chicago-based management consultants, absorbed so much knowledge while helping CN prepare its case for merger negotiations with CP that, after the talks collapsed, he proved invaluable to the privatization campaign.

Left: Blunt men with powerful egos drove the privatization campaign, and sometimes clashed. One CN insider says Edward C. Lumley, vice-chairman of Nesbitt Burns and a former federal Liberal cabinet minister, was "the glue that kept this thing together through some very tense periods."

Right: The shrewdness and experience of Nesbitt Burns deputy chairman, Gordon S. Lackenbauer, along with the company's clout in Canada, earned the investment bank a role as one of the three global coordinators of CN's IPO. PHOTO: JOËL BÉNARD

Top: On April 5, 1995, a CN train shot through the railway's new $190-million tunnel under the St. Clair River for the first time. The only link allowing double-stacked railcars to thunder straight through central Canada to the American midwest, the tunnel slashed the transit time between Halifax and Chicago by twenty-four hours.

Left: The solid reputation of W. David Wilson, president and deputy chief executive officer of ScotiaMcLeod, was one of several reasons why his firm became a global coordinator for the IPO.

Right: John O. Downing, a partner at Goldman, Sachs, New York, helped his firm win the CN "beauty contest"—and thus a role as the only American investment bank among the three global coordinators—by displaying what CN's Michael Sabia called "a cut-to-the-chase, get-the-hell-out-of-my-way attitude." PHOTO: PHOTOGRAPHIA

Left: Mark Tercek of Goldman, Sachs says, "I think we persuaded CN that we had the track record in privatization, the track record in rail deals, and the absolutely right people totally committed to it." PHOTO: DEBRA MINTER

Right: Craig Kloner of Goldman, Sachs was a rail analyst of such legendary ability that, according to CN Chairman David McLean, he alone was a major reason why CN recommended Goldman, Sachs to the government.

Top: Western Canada has long been CN's most profitable territory. From here, the railway hauls grain, grain products, forest products, coal, sulphur and fertilizer, mostly for export to Pacific nations and the U.S.

Left: Railway analysts are sleuths, salespeople and—most importantly from CN's point of view—storytellers. The corporation persuaded one of the best in the business, Gary Yablon of Schroder Wertheim, New York, to take a close look at CN's continuing turnaround.

Right: Winthrop B. Conrad Jr. of Davis Polk & Wardwell, New York, was the U.S. lawyer for CN. Conrad praised the Canadian government for the way it handled the privatization: "They saw that a really good commercial success would be a political success. And many governments don't perceive that in privatizations."

Right: CN hired Imagination Ltd., a London-based company that brings show-business timing and drama to corporate presentations, to produce a road show for potential investors. The project manager was Bernard Leibov of Imagination's Manhattan office, and the logistics manager for the gruelling tour of twenty-six cities in nine nations was Sarah Brennan.

On November 17, 1995, at stock exchanges in Toronto, Montreal and New York, CN shares traded for the first time. They were a phenomenal hit. At the Toronto Stock Exchange that afternoon, CN President Paul Tellier's smile told the story.

The Beauty Contest

Transport minister Doug Young wanted his staff involved in CN's privatization, and he wanted the finance department informed of the deal's progress. But he expected CN to prepare the deal, organize it, recommend the lead underwriters and work with them to pull it all off in record time. The underwriters' "beauty contest" therefore occurred before three CN judges: David McLean, Paul Tellier and Michael Sabia. The most persuasive executives from the great banking houses of Bay and Wall Streets trooped up to CN offices in Ottawa to parade the wares, talents and track records of their institutions.

"CN chose the big players, the global coordinators, early on," said rail analyst Gary H. Yablon, managing director of Schroder Wertheim & Co., New York, "and then added some others, including J.P. Morgan, Morgan Stanley and ourselves." Not until late summer was Schroder Wertheim invited aboard the privatization train, but as early as April, Yablon says, "I was spending a lot of time in Montreal, sucking up to them for this business. So were countless other investment firms. Because of its size, CN was courted by a great many people."

In judging a contestant, the CN triumvirate considered whether the firm had senior bankers with reputations for delivering the goods; a widely respected rail analyst on staff; a big sales force with the skill and experience to win orders from mighty institutional investors; and the savvy to have already developed solid ideas about how to promote the transaction.

"Of course, you always look for those sorts of things," Sabia says, "but because we wanted to do this in a way that had never been done before, we also wanted boldness, drive, *hunger*."

CN had a good relationship with Morgan Stanley, but in this contest, the venerable New York firm struck Sabia as a shade unaggressive. Not so John Downing of Morgan Stanley's powerful rival, Goldman, Sachs. "John came up here with a few of his guys, and he sat across the table from me," Sabia remembers, "and he said, 'Look, am I wasting my time here? Have you already decided you're gonna go with Morgan Stanley? Or do I have a chance of getting this account?' So I said to myself, 'I'm really interested in these people,' because there was a kind of cut-to-the-chase, get-the-hell-out-of-my-way attitude, and I thought, 'That's what you need to get this job done.' "

On May 5, the day Young introduced the CN Commercialization Act to the House of Commons, the government and CN board named the three global coordinators for the privatization: Goldman, Sachs, Nesbitt Burns, and ScotiaMcLeod. The two Canadian banks had worked closely with CN, but that wasn't as relevant to their selection as the talent and stature of some of their executives. At ScotiaMcLeod, these included President David Wilson and one of Canada's very few rail analysts, Vice-President Tony Hine (a college classmate of Michael Sabia's). The team at Nesbitt Burns included Vice-Chairman Ed Lumley and Deputy Chairman Gordon

Lackenbauer. Sabia regarded Lackenbauer, who headed the team, as "a *very* smart guy."

By Canadian standards, both banks had large, competent sales staffs. With $3.6 billion in underwritings and 16.4 per cent of Canada's market share in 1995, Nesbitt Burns was the country's top investment bank. ScotiaMcLeod stood fourth, with $2.7 billion in underwritings. "We thought it would be useful to bring in Scotia to debate issues with Nesbitt," Sabia says.

However big Nesbitt Burns and ScotiaMcLeod were in Canada, they were small beside Goldman, Sachs, which the *Economist* calls "arguably the world's most successful investment bank." In the year following CN's privatization, the pre-tax profits of this Wall Street giant reached US$2.6 billion, and it served as global coordinator and lead manager for international transactions worth US$31.8 billion. In thirty-two cities in seventeen nations, some 8,000 people work for Goldman, Sachs.

The bank has unbeatable experience in railway share offerings. It was the lead manager for the successful IPO of Consolidated Rail Corporation in the spring of 1987. It later handled so many offerings for other U.S. transportation companies that its top rail analyst, Craig Kloner, boasts, "We've done more IPOs and more secondary issues in the trucking and railway industries than all our competitors combined."

John Downing, whose hunger so impressed Sabia, was a seasoned authority on privatizations. "I've been doing these for years," he says. "I've worked with a lot of governments, mainly in the U.K. and Europe, and CN's must have been about my twenty-sixth privatization." The Goldman, Sachs CN-privatization team was headed by Mark Tercek, who reported to Downing. Tercek had worked on privatizations in Asia and had also run Goldman, Sachs's transportation group.

The third important Goldman, Sachs player in the CN privatization game was Kloner, an analyst of such legendary ability that, according to David McLean, he alone was a major reason why CN recommended Goldman, Sachs to the government. From the moment Kloner met McLean, Tellier and Sabia, he and his colleagues, unlike the Canadian bankers, expressed confidence to the point of cockiness that the privatization would be a hit.

"The success here," Kloner recalls, "was not only in taking what was a restructured company—operationally, managerially, financially—and putting it into the public marketplace, but also in convincing an enormous number of skeptics that it was not only doable, but doable at a far higher price and in a far more successful manner than any other investment bank thought possible, and I believe even the Canadian government thought possible."

"The only other 100 per cent rail IPO was ConRail, which we did," Tercek says, "and indeed, that was important. We knew firsthand that this could be accomplished. We drew a lot of lessons from the case of ConRail." At CN privatization meetings in Montreal, he says, "We pounded the table for debt reduction. We pounded the table for dividends, a large dividend. We pounded the table for stock options for management. We said it's critical to show potential investors that management will be incentivized to deliver, particularly when some of the managers come from the government sector . . . Those are the kinds of things we did."

Kloner staked his reputation on the deal. "When I gave my commitment during the so-called beauty contest that Goldman, Sachs could sell and would sell this stock, both in the United States and in Europe," he says, "it wasn't the Goldman, Sachs sales force commitment, it was *my personal commitment*."

"I said at the beginning," Sabia explains, "that I was not going to pre-agree the economics among the three global coordinators. What the Canadian banks wanted was an agreement that all three would make equal amounts. I said no, and they were extremely unhappy about that."

His reason for saying no was CN's desire to crack the U.S. market.

"I had to leave enough money there," he says. "I mean, realistically, Goldman, Sachs is a huge organization. They make money not by $1 million or $2 million, they make it by $10-, $20-, $30-, $40-million chunks. If I had hobbled their economics, this would have sunk to a low-priority deal for them. And that was a risk I couldn't take because the key to success was the U.S. market, and the U.S. market then triggering the Canadian market . . . There was a tremendous amount of conflict between me and the Canadian bankers over this. To this day, I'm probably burned in effigy in certain rooms in Toronto."

But with respect to how much Goldman, Sachs could earn from the deal, by comparison with other U.S. underwriters, CN *did* somewhat "hobble their economics." The way the American system works, the buyer of a chunk of stock gets to designate the investment bank that reaps the commission. But since the lead manager or "the book-runner," in this case Goldman, Sachs, allocates the stock, it has a powerful arm-twisting advantage. Especially when the deal is hot: *"You want stock? Well, you know who to designate for the commission, right?"*

Much as Sabia admired Goldman, Sachs, he did not want it to be the sole U.S. bank with "a tremendous incentive to go out and sell, sell, sell." He wanted as many messengers as possible telling the CN story, and the best were noted rail analysts like Gary Yablon of the relatively small Schroder Wertheim & Co. CN therefore imposed a cap on Goldman, Sachs's earnings from the privatization, and that, Sabia says, told other banks, "There's enough left in the pot here that Goldman, Sachs can't consume. If you do the work and get the designations, you've got a big payday coming."

The cap was 55 per cent of the selling concession in the U.S., and it was anathema to Goldman, Sachs.

Competition in investment banking is ferocious everywhere and tends to make its practitioners intensely loyal to their colleagues and institutions. This is true in Manhattan more than anywhere else. Young Wall Street millionaires like Tercek and Downing—

lean, clean-cut, clean-shaven, expensively shod and well tailored—not only speak reverently about each other ("Craig Kloner is a giant, simply a giant"), but exude a kind of distilled ambition for both themselves and their bank. The cap on Goldman, Sachs did not go down well with Downing. "John is fabulous," Sabia says. "He did a superb job for us, but you know, John is a *serious* guy. And hence, when I raised the issue of the cap, there was a lot of discussion between John and me. He wasn't all that enthusiastic about it."

A rail analyst who definitely was enthusiastic about the cap was Yablon of Schroder Wertheim. Limiting the amount of selling for which Goldman, Sachs could get paid in the U.S., Yablon said, was "very, very, *very* smart." To banks that wanted to compete for the money beyond the cap—banks like his—the arrangement said, "Jump ball!"

"It left these other guys really free to fight with each other," Yablon explains. "Fighting is the salespeople being aggressive, and the cap increased the incentive for these other guys to push the deal. It worked like a charm."

If CN was firm with Goldman, Sachs about the cap, Doug Young was firm about the commission for Canadian underwriters. In such deals, Sabia explains, "The economics are essentially pre-arranged in Canada. There's a fixed percentage, and that's that." The underwriters ran "this comfortable little cartel" with its own formula that set privatization commissions as low as 4 per cent, but no lower. The size of the CN deal, however, made it likely they would earn so much money that Young insisted—and he told Sabia to insist—on a better deal for Canada.

"The one thing nobody talked about is that we paid the lowest commission in Canadian history," Young boasts. "They [the investment bankers] didn't want this in the press." The rate was only 3.75 per cent. "[Young] got the toughest and tightest deal any government ever got," Lackenbauer said in May 1995.

"When they started to squeeze me on this," Young says, "I squeezed back. Everybody kept saying, 'You can't do this because it's a precedent,' but I said, '*Everything* we're doing here is a precedent, so why is this particular part of the precedent not acceptable?' But it all worked out, and I think they were happy in the end."

"Yeah," chuckles his executive assistant, Fred Drummie, "in the end."

McLean, too, spoke bluntly to the bankers. "I ended up being the guy who got tough with the brokers. I said, 'No more!' They were all in there—not so much Goldman, Sachs, but the Canadian brokers—they really wanted more and more and more, and finally somebody just had to say 'No!' "

Although the one American and two Canadian banks were equals as global coordinators, the government, on CN's advice, named Goldman, Sachs the lead manager internationally. The decision infuriated the bankers from Toronto. They were, after all, Canadians. CN was a Canadian enterprise. How could the Canadian government hand to an American bank the right to sell to European markets the shares of a Canadian crown corporation?

"The Canadian bankers used every possible mechanism to surface that issue in Ottawa with Paul Martin and others," Sabia says, "and to argue that we were doing the wrong thing here. They ended up not succeeding, but they were intensely unhappy." CN's position was that, though the Canadian banks could sell to the managers of Canadian equities working for European funds, that wasn't good enough. It wanted a far broader audience. It wanted the world to see it as a North American railway.

"Young asked me to compare the presence of Goldman, Sachs in Europe with that of Nesbitt Burns and ScotiaMcLeod," Sabia remembers, "and I said, 'Come on, one's *here* [lifting his right hand high above his head], and the others are here [lowering it to the tabletop] . . . Again, it was Young who agreed with our position and made it happen."

The anger of the Canadian banks was understandable, and

perhaps tinged with apprehension. Increasingly, gigantic international financial institutions were challenging Canadian investment banks on their own turf. Goldman, Sachs, Morgan Stanley, Merrill Lynch and others had hung out their shingles in downtown Toronto, competing with Canadian banks to get the business of any Canadian corporation that wanted to "go global." Along came what Sabia calls "a marquee privatization," the biggest in Canadian history, and what happened? Even though Scotia-McLeod and Nesbitt Burns felt they could handle the entire issue, the Canadian government named Goldman, Sachs their equal as a global coordinator; allowed it to take home more money from the deal than them; and also appointed it the lead manager in Europe.

In the war between the Canadian and international banks, Sabia says, "We were just one battle."

$900 Million:
No Trivial Decision

Despite the Canadian underwriters' anger over Goldman, Sachs's involvement in CN's privatization, relations between them and the U.S. bankers remained courteous throughout the spring, summer and early fall of 1995. They were all in the same business and shared the same jargon. They agreed on the crucial importance of the government slashing CN's debt before the Initial Public Offering and of the corporation selling its juicy downtown real estate in cities across the nation, including the CN Tower in Toronto. Unloading the real estate and what was left of the corporation's other non-rail assets would contribute mightily to the debt reduction, and also help make the IPO "a pure rail play."

The U.S. lines that had achieved the most miraculous turnarounds had become pure railways. Not only the CN underwriters, but other members of Paul Tellier's Tuesday-afternoon brain trust suspected that potential American investors would turn thumbs down on a railway whose extensive non-rail holdings distorted its focus.

"I kept telling Paul that the way to make the privatization work is to sell something to the market that the market understands," Torrance Wylie says. "Make it a pure rail play and address that operating ratio issue, and the market will be wildly enthusiastic. I said anything we do that compromises on that will cost us going out the door and could even put the privatization at risk. So that was going on in parallel with everything else: sell, sell, sell."

A political consideration also came into play. If the value of the real estate rose sharply after the privatization, and if CN then sold the properties piece by hugely profitable piece, they would amount to a windfall for the corporation and its shareholders, and an embarrassment to a government that hadn't been smart enough to keep them.

None of these arguments, however, convinced Chairman David McLean that selling CN's property was a good idea. He knew the real estate business better than Doug Young, Tellier or any of their advisers, and his fierce opposition to CN selling off its non-rail assets endeared him to neither the corporation nor the transport minister. Indeed, McLean's resistance ignited what one Tellier adviser called "a huge battle."

Concerning this time, McLean says, "I had a very strange relationship with Doug Young. I was appointed by the prime minister, and I don't think Doug ever accepted the fact that I wasn't his appointment." Young resented McLean taking his disagreements about the privatization plan to the prime minister, but McLean believed Jean Chrétien had given him "a mandate to make sure we ended up with a deal that was good for everybody."

To strain the relationship further, McLean acknowledges, "I had a lot of very strong views myself. At first, I didn't think we should sell the real estate because I felt we were selling the heritage of the company. We had our differences on that." He was not alone. As a crown corporation, CN had long been selling subsidiaries and divisions to cover cash requirements, and some still saw its valuable urban properties as insurance against inevitable bad times.

"It was a major difference," Tellier says. "The point Michael [Sabia] and I were making was that it's very nice to have a cushion, but it's more important to reduce the debt as much as possible. We're better off to give the government [the non-rail real estate] and at the same time have the government apply it to our debt reduction. Doug Young believed in this strongly, and needless to say, it was Doug Young who carried the day."

But not easily.

"I had more trouble with [real estate] probably than I did structuring the consortium," Young remembers, "what with people trying to hang onto it or take it out with them when CN went. And with other people thinking we weren't getting fair value, that it wasn't being appraised properly."

McLean eventually agreed that the best thing to do with the real estate was sell it, mainly because "the price was right."

In December 1994, when the privatization of CN was in the wind but not a declared goal, CP decided to reveal just how much money the crown corporation had cost Canadian taxpayers since its birth. As CP informed the Liberals' task force on CN's commercialization, "Through much of its history, CN's interest expenses and capital expenditures have been far out of balance with its earning power. In the private sector, it would have failed many times over. The cumulative effect has been substantial—amounting to $96 billion [in 1993 dollars]."

But Yvon Masse, CN's chief financial officer until 1995, had an answer to CP's claim. He says that if one added up the value of all the assets and resources donated to CP since its founding, and then "charged that total cumulatively at compound interest rates, to the government, the figure might even exceed $100 billion." The $96 billion was merely an example of CP's "fancy games." As speculation increased about the cost of the CN privatization, business

journalists freely tossed about that damning figure, rarely acknowl-
edging its source, or that CN had received not a nickel of subsidy
during the previous seventeen years, or indeed that it had actually
paid the government more than $200 million in dividends.

By mid-February 1995, CN's debt had shot back up to $2.5 billion,
and CP was campaigning against any privatization that might see the
government hold on to a big chunk of the debt. What CP opposed was
a major bailout, not privatization per se. Indeed, Robert Ritchie,
who took over as CP Rail's chief executive in March, welcomed CN to
the private sector. "We'll still be competitors," said Ritchie, "but
the wind for them will be the same for us, and it hasn't been that way
for seventy-odd years."

On the other hand, Ritchie argued, CN's $2.5 billion in loans was
not just old debt. "They bought an awful lot of assets with those
debts," he said. CN had been spending so aggressively its indebtedness had jumped 40 per cent in just two years, and thanks to the
government's backing its credit like a rich uncle, the railway now
boasted "a dowry of high-quality assets." Ritchie worried about a
government bailout that would give the newly privatized corporation an unfair advantage. "We would start to get a little anxious if
any more than $200 million of CN debt was forgiven," he said on
May 6, 1995. The enrichment of CN, just to get a successful share
issue on the market, "would have an immediate impact on CP Rail's
ability to raise capital. The competitive implications are obvious."

Truckers' organizations joined CP in opposing a major government recapitalization of CN. "There's a hyper-competitive market
in freight transportation already," said David Bradley of the
Ontario Trucking Association. "It's not too many companies that
can recapitalize at the public's expense."

Not only CN's competitors, but even some senior bureaucrats
were deeply uneasy about how much the government would sink into
the corporation before putting it on the market. In the end, Paul
Martin and Doug Young settled the matter; they made yet another of
the bold and politically risky decisions that ensured the privatiza-

tion's success. The feds agreed to make a $900-million equity contri-
bution to CN for debt reduction, while CN transferred hundreds of
millions of dollars worth of real estate to Ottawa. By selling other
assets, CN would eliminate further debts of $500 million. The total
debt reduction of $1.4 billion lowered the corporation's annual inter-
est payments by $100 million, and a 1995 asset write-down of $1.3
billion cut annual depreciation costs by a further $59 million.

The restructured, privatized corporation would have long-term
debts totalling $1.35 billion. Its debt-to-capitalization ratio would
be under 40 per cent. That was good by the standards of U.S. railways, and low enough for CN to earn the investment-grade credit
rating it required to intrigue potential buyers of the stock.

"The Canadian transportation industry reacted with disgust
yesterday to the government's write-down of a substantial debt of
[CN] as part of its IPO," the *Financial Post* reported on August 29.
Much of the disgust came from CP. "This is a *de facto* recapitalization at taxpayers' expense," said CP Rail spokesman B. C. Scott.
"No matter how you cut it, $900 million works out to a recapital-
ization and we were not subject to those benefits."

Other critics of the debt-reduction program often failed to grasp
what it was actually buying. "Bozos in the business press said the
government was throwing good money after bad," Gordon Lackenbauer recalls. To a reporter grilling him by phone, he said, "Look, if
you have a house for sale, and it has a 95 per cent mortgage on it,
and the real-estate experts say you'll get a far better price if you
reduce the mortgage to 45 per cent, what do you do?" By making
CN more marketable, the debt reduction guaranteed more money,
not less, would flow to Ottawa. Even after paying out the $900 mil-
lion, Ottawa would pocket at least $1 billion, Lackenbauer insisted,
and also reap the real estate.

Leaving aside marketing tactics, CN executives felt the $900 mil-
lion was certainly not an overpayment for the real estate, plus all the
debts that government policies had forced upon the corporation.
The Newfoundland Railway, to take but one example, had cost CN

more than $700 million. When the government chose to invest a last
$900 million in the privatization, CN therefore did not feel it was get-
ting something for nothing. "We only got what was owed, deserved
and required," says Wes Kelley, vice-president, public affairs and
advertising.

"When we were restructuring the debt," Young remembers, "people were saying, 'Holy smokes, you'll be paying them to take it off
our hands!' Nobody would believe we'd net out the kind of money
we did. But we had to do the restructuring regardless of all that,
and with no pricing [of the shares], so we were going ahead blind.
We kept worrying about getting the right rating from the bond-
rating agencies, and whatnot."

The size of CN's indebtedness and its debt-capitalization ratio,
Wylie explains, were "hugely significant for values down the road."
Paying off debt to get those numbers right, and then expecting to
recover the payment in the share price made eminent sense, he continues, "_But try and sell that in Ottawa_. It's just not what people are
familiar with. Again, you see, Doug made the right decision."

It was the bankers who recommended the government inject
$900 million into CN, but it was Young and Martin who had the
chutzpa to turn the advice into reality.

"That was a critically, critically important decision in terms of
rating the company financially," Sabia says. "No one thought we'd
be able to get $900 million to do that, and indeed most of the pub-
lic servants didn't think we would—or _should_—get it. It was those
two ministers who said, 'We're going to do what we have to do to
make this thing a success. And if that means we got to kick in an
extra $200 million [on top of the figure they were discussing], and
you bankers tell us we'll get that back . . . Well, you better be
damn sure we _do_ get it back, but if that's your advice, we're willing
to do it.' And for a minister of finance, that was no trivial decision,
to say the least. But he made it, and it worked out, and the government did in fact get paid that much more."

The $900-million decision, Sabia believes, was further proof that Martin and Young wanted "no more half-hearted, hand-wringing, cautious, Canadian privatizations. Companies have been privatized in Canada before, but none of them in the bold way this one was done."

Right Board, Right Rules

O f all Doug Young's privatization achievements, the one that made him proudest was giving CN a superior board of directors.

"The most important thing Doug did," Paul Martin says, "was immediately go out and get CN as good a board as it has. That was enormously important. It gave the whole thing credibility." For more than seven decades, governments had been packing CN's board with loyalists, bagmen and failed politicians from whichever old-line party happened to be in power. That was a major reason why the business community could never take the corporation seriously. If there was one thing upon which David McLean and the Paul Tellier brain trust entirely agreed it was the importance of appointing a *real* board of reputable business leaders—and doing it well before the Initial Public Offering.

Why would a business luminary want to become a director of such a "sleepy pig" as CN? For Cedric E. Ritchie, then the sixty-eight-year-old chairman of the executive committee of the Bank of Nova Scotia, the answer lay in something as simple as love of country. "I was always intrigued by railways," says Ritchie. "They're part of the history of Canada. And I guess we're all kids at heart." And Purdy Crawford says, "It was just one month before I ceased to be the CEO [at Imasco]. I thought I had the time, and it was a very exciting thing to get involved in."

"It was a two-way street," Young says. "First, I had to get the prime minister to understand why we wanted to do it—he accepted it, no problem—and then I had to persuade these people to come on. When we told them what we were doing, and that their appointments wouldn't be just perfunctory or ceremonial —'We want you *pushing* here'—their enthusiasm was fantastic."

By the early summer of 1995, CN had its new board. It included McLean, Tellier, Ritchie, Crawford and J.V. Raymond Cyr, chairman, Bell Canada, Montreal; V. Maureen Kempston Darkes, president and general manager, General Motors of Canada, Toronto; Jean B. Forest, president, J.B.F. Holdings, Edmonton; Richard H. Kroft, president, Tryton Investment Company, Winnipeg; Denis Losier, president and CEO, Assumption Life, and former New Brunswick cabinet minister, Moncton; Dr. Edward P. Neufeld, visiting senior research fellow, University of Toronto, and a former executive vice-president, Royal Bank; and Robert Pace, president, the Pace Group, Halifax.

"I'll tell you what," Young says. "If I was returning to the private sector tomorrow, and I had these people on my board, I'd be the luckiest guy in Canada."

The board gave CN fresh lustre in the eyes of potential investors, but as Young had promised, it served as more than an ornament. The members brought their formidable judgement to bear on all the bigger privatization issues, and attended not only the monthly gatherings of the full board, but the meetings of six different committees. The privatization group met regularly all through the summer and fall of 1995.

Purdy Crawford served as chairman of the human resources committee. It wrestled with the tricky issue of executives' salaries, which had to be competitive but not high enough to arouse public indignation, and worked on the arrangements whereby all employees could buy CN stock, as well as the stock incentives for executives.

American investors, in particular, would want to see the rewards to senior managers tied directly to CN's performance. With the help of Crawford and his committee, CN devised an unusual plan: executives eligible for the Management Matching Offer would receive options to buy common shares at the initial offering price, yet would not be able to exercise two thirds of the options *unless CN's operating ratio dropped from 85.6 per cent in 1996 to 82 per cent in the year 2000*. Guaranteeing that the more efficient CN became, the richer its bosses would get, the scheme was not only a promising idea in its own right, but a major selling point in the U.S.

"Wall Street analysts love to have things simple," Craig Kloner says. That was the beauty of an incentive plan with specific targets. "Every outside observer could say, 'Oh, so this is where the profit margin could be, because that's where the incentive is,' " he explains. " 'Oh my goodness, this is cheap.' Analysts love to be spoonfed, so they were spoonfed."

When Crawford attended his first CN board meeting in early summer, he wondered how the privatization could possibly be achieved by fall. "There were a lot of people there, including consultants," he recalls, "and all the things that had to be done were outlined: all the way from revaluing the assets and writing them down, to negotiating with the government on the transfer of the real estate back to the crown, getting settlements on Indian lands, all that. And I remember thinking to myself—not saying it out loud because it's the last thing any director wants to hear—'God, this is an impossible schedule.' "

Some CN staff knew that if the schedule was not impossible, it was certainly punishing. Remembering the advice of former Air

Canada Chairman Claude Taylor and others—about the importance of cracking open the culture of a crown corporation bound for privatization—Tellier in late July ordered Louise Piché, CN's vice-president, quality and human resources, to design a half-day course to introduce 1,800 first-line supervisors to business principles. He gave her only two weeks, and she postponed her vacation plans.

"We turned the world over," Piché says. "While designing the course and producing its printed material, a lot of people worked 'round the clock, they were so challenged by the job thrown at us. In two weeks we had it ready to launch." The course took classes of eighteen to twenty employees through the life of an imaginary bicycle rental company and gave them a speedy understanding of profit, net revenue, cash flow, depreciation, fixed and variable costs, return on investment and other business concepts. Between mid-August and late September, some 1,400 employees completed the course. Simply organizing the classes, Piché says, was "a massive logistical task."

The privatization drive thrust extra work not only on Piché's staff, but on the whole railway. During this period, CN employees were running the railroad, enduring downsizing and digging out information their superiors required to prepare the privatization pitch. To support the merger negotiations with CP, and then to react knowledgeably to CP's bid to buy CN East, staff had assembled rafts of statistics in 1994 and unearthed an unprecedented body of information about CN's assets. Launched well before anyone talked seriously about the privatization of CN, this work would prove essential to the government's ability to sell CN as early as November 1995. So, however, would a backbreaking burden of fresh work for managers and staff.

Each major privatization decision that CN and the government reached imposed on the corporation's work force more responsibilities, headaches and working hours. "Just about everyone around here was putting in fifteen-hour days," says Wes Kelley. "We joked about it a lot. We'd say, 'Let's go down to the lobby and count the body bags.' "

From the decision to list the shares on the New York Stock Exchange, to take just one example, flowed several work streams. "Not many Canadian companies are on the New York exchange, and none was ever there on Day One," says Claude Mongeau, now vice-president, strategic and financial planning. "So what does it take to get there? You've got to have a full prospectus, and you've got to go to the Securities and Exchange Commission down there. You cannot overestimate the amount of work involved. It's a wonder we ever got on the New York exchange. We had to redefine the world.

"There were a whole number of criteria we didn't meet because, as a crown corporation, we'd never made any money. Our people in accounting had to redo all our financial statements for the Americans. So day-to-day, we'd be pushing the accounting department, pushing our U.S. lawyer to get the exemptions and working with the investment banks on the prospectus and the securities issues we had to deal with."

To take a later example, CN had a team handling "the largest debt-defeasance program in the history of Canada . . . All of this took our treasurer and his staff four or five months of hard work, real hard work."

The offices of Sabia and Mongeau were "the central command post, managing consultants and the internal people, coordinating the work, pushing, pushing, pushing . . ." To complete the prospectus, Mongeau continues, they had to get "the whole organization" to agree on priorities and objectives, and also obtain detailed answers to big questions: How did CN's performance stack up beside those of U.S. railways? How could it close the gap and by how much?

"Within a strategic planning framework," Mongeau says, "the entire operating side and marketing side of CN had to provide information so that the investment bankers, and everybody around the table, would believe we really had a plan to get there. We were posting aggressive targets, and the bankers had to feel satisfied they were real."

Only once did Mongeau throw up his hands. Sabia worked such long hours that a New York banker once joked, "I think his wife forgot what he looked like." During many of Sabia's most exhausting days at CN headquarters, Mongeau was at his side. At 10:30 one night in late June, they were working in Sabia's office overlooking the St. Lawrence River. Above the Jacques Cartier Bridge, huge fireworks blossomed, their reflections exploding on the calm surface of the river. The two men watched for a while, and then, Mongeau remembers, "I sat down and I said, 'Michael, it isn't possible. We won't make it in '95. It's got to be into '96. It's just impossible.'

"There was just *so much*, but we said we will do it *all*. And we won't compromise. And a small miracle—we did it. And we never compromised, and it was a big success."

With the privatization sprint well under way, the government advanced on two other fronts to impose drastic change on Canada's railway industry. First, it abolished the ninety-eight-year-old "Crow's Rate" system, whereby Transport Canada, at a cost that had reached $560 million a year, subsidized the shipping of grain by rail from the Prairies to Pacific ports and to Thunder Bay, Ontario. To ease the pain for Prairie farmers, who faced a sharp jump in freight rates with the cancellation of the Crow, the government distributed among them a one-shot payment of $1.6 billion.

The *Journal of Commerce*, widely read by American railway executives, reported that Canadian bureaucrats said the elimination of the subsidies was essential "to create a more efficient system for shippers and carriers, as well as to comply with new world trading rules that impose substantial dollar and volume restrictions on trade-distorting export subsidies." Abolishing the subsidies would hasten the closure of unprofitable rail lines and the launching of unit trains.

On June 20, 1995, the same day the CN Commercialization Act received its third and final reading, the government introduced legislation to improve what bankers liked to call the "environment" in which Canadian railways operated. The new Canada Transportation Act would, at long last, help free CN and CP from the bureaucratic hassles they endured whenever they tried to shed a money-losing line. With respect to the ease with which a railway could rid itself of lines, the Staggers Act had given the U.S. railways a fifteen-year head start on CN and CP. Canada's National Transportation Act (NTA) of 1987 had proved a financial disaster for Canadian railways. "The NTA was the Canadian government's half-witted attempt to inject competition into the industry," business journalist Andrew Osterland wrote in *Financial World*. "It was great for shippers but a disaster for railroads. Although it deregulated freight rates on the revenue side of the equation, it did nothing to facilitate network rationalization on the cost side. Predictably, profits plummeted."

CN and CP spent years trying to abandon or sell some lines. The process was so expensive and complicated, they were often discouraged from even trying. In 1993, the National Transportation Act Review Commission, whose report Tellier called "a blueprint for the survival of Canada's railway industry," urged the government to complete the job of deregulation by making it easier for the railways to discard track. In 1994, the Nault task force recommended "a more expedient processing of abandonment applications and transfers of lines to new operators," as well as "an orderly shedding of uneconomic assets." In 1995, Robert Ritchie, CEO of CP Rail, said, "I would bend down and kiss the ground if the Canadian government would introduce legislation like the Staggers Act."

The Canadian Transportation Act, as it turned out, would not grant Canadian railways as much freedom as the Staggers Act had given the American lines, but Tellier nevertheless welcomed it as "a first step in moving Canada's railways and their customers closer to regulatory parity with their U.S. competitors."

Under the old legislation, CP and CN had to apply to the National Transportation Agency to abandon a line or sell it to a short-line operator. "You had to show you were losing money on the line," Sabia explains. "Now notice: *losing money*, as opposed to not earning a commercial return. Big difference. And second, if you *were* losing money, that bureaucratic process could also say, 'Yes, you're losing money, but there's a public interest served by the operation of that line, so you shall continue to run it, but we'll give you a subsidy to do so.' So it was a bureaucratized process, not driven by commercial principles."

The new rules were much different. They stipulated that a railway must advertise its intention to shed a line. If no short-line operator expressed an interest, and if no agency of government—federal, provincial or municipal—made an offer before a certain deadline, then the railway could simply walk away from the line.

"So if one of those levels of government really thinks there's some huge public purpose in having this line, well, they can put their money where their mouth is and buy it," Sabia continues. "There's no bureaucratic oversight. We don't have to prove whether we're losing money or not losing money. If we think we're not earning an adequate return on that line, or we don't want to operate it, or whatever, we just put it in the public domain, and if somebody buys it, somebody buys it, and if nobody does, we abandon it. The whole process has been streamlined. It's much, much better."

The Canada Transportation Act would not have the force of law until July 1, 1996, but in the fall of 1995, everyone considering an investment in CN knew it was coming. Privatization insiders would later argue that the five phenomena that made the deal so marketable were: the pending improvement in the regulatory environment; the arbitrated labour settlement that took into account the "economic viability" of the railways; the appointment of one of the best boards in Canada; the financial restructuring that included lopping $1.4 billion off the corporation's debt; and the extent to which Tellier, Sabia and their team had already proved they had the drive to bulldoze CN through a U.S.-style turnaround.

CHAPTER 13

With a Drumroll
or a Bang?

For everyone who wanted CN's Initial Public Offering to succeed, certain events were gifts from the
blue. In February 1995, the month that finance
minister Paul Martin announced the railway's privatization in his
budget, the shareholders of Burlington Northern Inc. and Santa Fe
Pacific Corp. approved a merger of their two companies, thereby
creating the biggest rail carrier in North America. Burlington
Northern bought Santa Fe for an estimated US$2.5 billion. Then
Union Pacific Corp. bought 100 per cent of the common stock of
Chicago & North Western Transportation Co.—a deal worth about
US$1.2 billion. The first merger gave the Santa Fe shareholders a
handsome premium on their investment, and the second did the
same for the stockholders of C&NW.

"So there was a warm feeling among railroad investors that they
had just made a lot of money," says James M. Foote, a former execu-

tive of C&NW. "And the way these portfolios work, if a fund is performing well and its manager has so much of it invested in railroads, and if he wants to keep his portfolio properly balanced, well, he's looking for *another* railroad to invest in." At exactly the right moment, CN rolled clickety-clack into the market.

It was also at exactly the right moment that Foote joined CN. He was still a high-school boy when he got his first railroad job, shovelling sewers in a roundhouse in Superior, Wisconsin. He studied law at night school in Chicago and dug ditches by day for C&NW before joining its labour relations and corporate secretary's offices. During his two decades at C&NW, Foote helped battle the United Transportation Union; served as tax vice-president; ran the offices of corporate development, and investor and public relations; participated in a leveraged buyout, two public offerings of shares and three road shows for investors; and in his own words, was "on a team that had to terminate a third of the management in one day, just to assuage the equity markets."

In August 1995, after Union Pacific bought C&NW, CN welcomed Foote as its vice-president, investor relations. He was only forty-one, but few people better knew the institutional investors in U.S. railways, the bankers who specialized in railroad deals and the rail analysts at brokerage houses. Just as CN put the finishing touches on the preliminary prospectus that would guide its charge towards the IPO, it hired the youngest "grizzled veteran" in the business.

"The time is 1978, the scene a decrepit, weed-choked U.S. railroad yard," Mark Hallman wrote in the *Financial Post* in July 1995. "A motionless freight car spontaneously derails as rusting rails and rotting ties give way. More then 20 per cent of U.S. railroads are insolvent and face nationalization. Investors consider them a write-off.

"Fast forward to 1995 to a state-of-the-art railroad intermodal terminal bursting at the seams with truck trailers and containers on flat cars. U.S. rail assets are in the best shape ever, and rail

market share is rising. Investors are enamoured with record earnings, surplus cash flows and potential for still more gains."

Thus, Hallman highlighted the railway industry revolution that
had swept the U.S. What many Canadian investment "experts" did
not know—and did not trouble themselves to find out—was that
CN was no longer in the weed-choked yard, but had joined this same
revolution. Following the hard example of those U.S. lines, the corporation had stuck to a fierce schedule of cost-cutting. Indeed, CN
was driving the last cost-driven railway turnaround in North
America. If there was a best-kept secret in Canadian industry in
mid-1995, it was that CN, unlike Air Canada and Petro-Canada
before their privatizations, was already intriguing institutions with
tens of millions of dollars to invest.

The only transcontinental railway in North America, it had double-stack capacity from coast to coast, the continent's best-balanced mix of rail freight and the highest proportion of long-haul,
high-volume traffic. CN served every major Canadian port and
boasted the most direct route between Chicago and Toronto-Mon-
treal. Trains were now zooming through its new tunnel at Sarnia-
Port Huron, the only one able to move double-stack containers
between Canada and the U.S. CN was a world leader in railway information technology. It carried 130 million tons of freight a year and
in 1994 collected rail revenues of more than $4.3 billion.

None of this, however, was as eye-opening as its unsung record
as a slasher of costs. CN's chopping of 11,000 jobs was on schedule
for completion in 1995. "I know of no other company in this country achieving cost reductions on the scale CN is achieving them,"
Wes Kelley, vice-president, public affairs and advertising, said in an
internal memo. "We have been extracting labour costs at the rate of
something like $15 million a month for the past two years."

The streamlining of CN had included the reduction of shop
capacity by 35 per cent, of management layers from as many as
twelve to five, regional headquarters from five to two, and labour
costs from 47 per cent of revenue to 41 per cent. CN had abandoned

several hundred kilometres of low-density track and sold two unprofitable lines, as well as a profitable oil and gas subsidiary.

It had accomplished all this while increasing both productivity and traffic volume. Between 1992 and 1994, that all-important operating ratio dropped from more than 97 percent to 90.1 and continued to decline in 1995. In 1994, CN racked up the best improvement in profits in the North American rail industry. At $245 million, they still weren't as high as they would have to rise, but the downward slide had started to swing uphill. These were the best profits CN had delivered in six years.

Investors who studied the preliminary prospectus CN filed with securities commissions on August 28, 1995, might have gathered that the railway was rocketing towards new levels of efficiency. And if they knew the full story of the railway turnarounds south of the border, they would have surmised that all CN had to do, to become a hot competitor in its own right, was keep right on copying what its toughest U.S. rivals had done: slash costs, jack up service and employ assets ever more efficiently.

"We could go out and tell the Americans, 'Look, we're not geniuses,' " Michael Sabia says. " 'We're just doing what your own railroads have done with great success.' And they'd say, 'Yeah, we've seen this story before.' "

Railway-smart U.S. investors knew the industry CEOs in their own country. "But they didn't have a clue who these guys from Canada were," James Foote says. "So our goal was to go down there and say, 'Hey, we're just like the U.S. guys.' So we develop the information the same way the U.S. guys do. Everything looks the same. We look like a U.S. railroad. We talk like a U.S. railroad. That was very much the strategy."

While touting the new board of directors, new management team, new debt-equity ratio, new collective agreements and impending regulatory changes, CN could also show the Americans the giant steps it had already taken to drive down costs.

"Our message was very simple," Sabia explains. "We said, 'Look we've taken 11,000 employees out of this company. You can construct your own model to see what that's going to mean. We're just waiting for the financial impact of these cuts. How can you lose? All we're asking you to do is enjoy the ride.' This was the real financial driver."

The three global underwriters understood why this strategy would work. Indeed, Goldman, Sachs, with its unparalleled experience in share offerings for U.S. railways, had promoted it way back in March, during CN's beauty contest for underwriters. Many Canadian investment dealers, federal bureaucrats and business journalists, however, were less sanguine.

Although the corporation's employees were quietly confident that a privatized CN could compete successfully against American railways, CP and truckers, it seemed that scarcely anyone else in Canada was. "We had a board meeting in Winnipeg in the summer of '95," Kelley recalls, "and I sat with one of the Transport Canada people at dinner that night, and it was very clear they did not think the privatization would succeed."

Right up until the preliminary prospectus appeared, and even after, the sneering continued in Canadian newspapers. Commentators still saw CN as a bloated creature, chronically haemorrhaging taxpayers' money and forever wallowing in the wasteful culture of a crown corporation. Often, the journalists were parroting off-the-cuff remarks by doubtful bankers. An underwriter friend of Gordon Lackenbauer asked him, "Do you really think you can sell that dog?" In short, the view was widespread in Canada that the privatization would be at best a disappointment and at worst an investment and political disaster.

Although the history both of CN and of previous privatizations in Canada and abroad underlay much of the general skepticism (Ed Lumley thought "the Canadian psyche" also had something to do with it), certain terms of the deal aroused specific criticism. Some commentators were angered, for instance, that CN's headquarters would remain in Montreal; others didn't like the fact that no single buyer could ever own more than 15 per cent of CN stock. "That will discourage buyers," the *Globe and Mail* declared in an editorial, "particularly foreign buyers, who might want to run the railway, not just invest in it."

It baffled CN's Canadian underwriters that Canadian editorial writers and business columnists often failed to phone people who knew what was going on, but simply shot off their mouths. According to Lackenbauer, the underwriters all knew "that 15 per cent of such a large market cap would not deter the institutional investors, not one bit, and would have zero impact on the price."

Gerald Davies, the senior vice-president, marketing, whom Paul Tellier had lured away from Burlington Northern in 1993, encountered "phenomenal" pessimism about CN's future in Canada's government and newspapers. "You look at the demand for rail properties in Argentina, Mexico, Britain, Australia, New Zealand," he says, "and here you've got one with good engines, cars and track, with a great industrial base, and it feeds its industrial neighbour in the most efficient way imaginable—and to think it doesn't have a *future*. It's unfathomable. I couldn't believe it. I just shook my head. This railway was a winner. If it wasn't a winner, I wouldn't have come up here."

The forecasts proved to be so wrong-headed that, after the closing of the IPO, an article in *Railway Age* entitled "Canadian National privatization confounds the media" declared that the deal had left "Canada's business writers and analysts with egg on their faces."

In view of CN's history and the ignorance in Canada about railway investment, Tellier says the bad press was forgivable. He remembers it without bitterness. Davies, however, says, "I know it hurt Tellier at the time. You pour your heart and soul into something, seven days a week for three years, and then somebody writes all that, and you *know* it's all wrong."

The media hammering was also unnerving for some of Tellier's most trusted advisers. "There were an awful lot of articles that said there'd be no buyers for CN," Torrance Wylie says. "So just imagine the guys like myself. We'd said, 'Don't worry, there's a big public market out there for this company.' Then you start reading this stuff, and you wonder, 'Have we been wrong all along?' "

What particularly frustrated CN was that, throughout most of the summer of 1995, the corporation had to endure the pummelling without defending itself. Once Paul Martin had announced the privatization, everyone involved with it, in Canada and the U.S., was working within "the quiet period." Any serious violation of the quiet period, which lasted until the sale was complete, might have invited both the American and Canadian securities commissions to slap orders on the IPO, postponing or even scuttling the whole deal.

The purpose of the quiet period is to discourage the trumpeting of rosy predictions about the company being sold, the broadcasting of sunny projections of earnings or otherwise hyping the stock.

"If you want to sell securities, you must follow a very defined set of rules," says Jean-Pierre Ouellet, CN's Canadian lawyer during the privatization and later its chief legal officer and corporate secretary. "Unless otherwise exempted, you must produce a prospectus, and the prospectus is really the warranties and presentations you make about the company. It's supposed to be the truth, the whole truth and nothing but the truth . . . Now the rule during the quiet period—and this is putting it in perhaps an oversimplified way—is that you should try to arouse interest in the security you're selling *only* through the use of that prospectus."

Stepping carefully through this quiet period was such a serious matter that, at one point, Kelley doubted whether Tellier should keep an appointment with editors of the *Financial Post*. "The fact that you will not be on the record, and that you are meeting with them as do many other business leaders, does not change the fact that you are visiting a financial news publication," Kelley warned the CEO. "Jean-Pierre [Ouellet] believes that if the Ontario Securities Commission hears about it, the possibility of an adverse response is high. He feels that rumours travel too fast and too far for the visit to remain a secret."

The regulators of the securities commissions, however, are not invariably rigid in their demand that the prospectus be the only selling tool. They pounce on promoters who break the rule openly and systematically, but according to Ouellet, would not have worried about a CN executive phoning a journalist and saying, "Hey, you wrote this and that, and you might have been right three years ago, but we're over the hump now, and if you're going to write about us again, would you check your story a little better?"

The regulators' flexibility left room for testiness between, on the one hand, Kelley and the publicity professionals in his corner, and on the other, Ouellet and CN's American lawyer, Winthrop B. Conrad Jr. Arguing that the quiet period need not be a *silent* period, Kelley wanted to counter the bad publicity by subtly spreading accurate and positive information about the corporation even before the preliminary prospectus appeared.

"And Paul [Tellier] and Michael [Sabia], to their credit, wanted to do everything possible to make sure the deal was successful," Conrad explains. "They didn't want to wait until the last minute to draw out the market, and I think they were skeptical that, as someone called it, 'this boring old prospectus' would be able to do it. But in [the U.S.], it *does* do it . . . Goldman, Sachs wanted only the prospectus and the road show. That's all. They said, 'We will sell it on that alone. We don't need all this other stuff.' It was hard for CN to accept this concept, and I think they were doing their job in trying to push the issue as far as it could be pushed."

Both Conrad and Ouellet, however, were adamant that, though CN might get away with what Kelley proposed, the benefit just wouldn't be worth the risk of a crackdown by securities commissions. The argument became so heated at one meeting, Kelley recalls, "Conrad told me that if I did in his country what I was trying to do in mine, I'd go to jail."

In late August, just before CN filed its preliminary prospectus with Canadian securities commissions and a registration statement with the U.S. Securities and Exchange Commission, an argument erupted at CN over how to publicize the document. "We had a torrid meeting over this," Kelley says. "I remember Cedric Ritchie was there from the board, and Ed Lumley, Goldman, Sachs, Nesbitt Burns, ScotiaMcLeod, A. T. Kearney, the lawyers. It was like Noah's ark. In they came, two-by-two."

The lawyers urged that on August 28, the day CN was to file the prospectus, the corporation distribute one fat press release on the whole story of the financial restructuring, sale of the real estate, write-down of assets, management incentive plan, employee share purchase plan and financial results for the second quarter of 1995. This seemed the most discreet way to distribute important news during the quiet period. Kelley, however, argued that starting to release information about the financial restructuring would at last arouse some genuine media interest and that giving the entire story away in "one big bang" was a mistake. "Having awakened the media beast," he says, "we'd have nothing to feed it. I wanted not the big bang, but a drumroll of releases. We were overruled."

Worried that the media might misinterpret the release, which ran to nine pages, CN held "a news briefing lock-up with selected financial journalists" rather than a full-scale press conference. Since even this low-key event made the lawyers uneasy, CN banned tape recorders and invited only journalists who had previously originated stories on the privatization. To make sure no CN official gave a risky answer to a journalist's question, Jean-Pierre Ouellet sat in on the briefing.

Although CN was among the biggest industries in Montreal, the Montreal *Gazette* had relied exclusively on wire services for its coverage of the story, and the railway therefore excluded it. The organizations represented included the *Globe and Mail, Financial Post, La Presse, Les Affaires, Financial Times* of London, *Journal of Commerce* and Dow Jones News Service. "This meeting was useful," Kelley says, "but as I had foreseen, we soon had nothing else to say, and people began to chew on us."

Some argued later that media predictions about a dreadful investment led to the government setting the share price so low it cost Canadians millions of dollars. Ouellet suggests the business press, no matter what it forecast, had little influence. "With an issue in excess of $2 billion, the success won't depend on the retail market," he says. "It's not you or me buying 100, 500, 1,000 or even 5,000 shares that will make the issue a success. It's the institutional investors buying huge blocks worth millions of dollars, and the analysts with the big mutual funds, or the big brokerage houses that do their own homework. They'll reach their own conclusions. These are sophisticated investors—and not likely to be deterred by negative newspaper articles."

They weren't.

On the Road
and Over the Sea

C N's new directors boarded a freight train at
Kamloops, British Columbia, one morning in
September 1995, seated themselves in a rear-
end observation car previously used by royalty, and for ten hours
rolled through spectacular mountain scenery and down to the sea at
Vancouver. There they enjoyed a sunset tour of the harbour, dined
at a banquet and attended one of their monthly board meetings. CN
advisers, bankers, rail analysts and senior managers went along for
the ride. Although some CN executives had complained they were
too busy for this jaunt, Chairman David McLean had insisted on it.

"Everyone was getting very ratty at this stage," he explains.
"The company was under intense pressure, and we had to do something to relieve it. Also, the board had not yet coalesced. People
didn't really know one another. Bringing everybody out of Montreal, getting out here and actually seeing the railway in action—it

was a great coming-together. After that, everybody respected one another. There was less tension in the air. It was just terrific."

If the trip gladdened the hearts of CN privatization promoters in September, so did the government's hugely successful sale of most of the Petro-Canada shares it still owned. The *Financial Post* called the deal "the most welcome sale of the past decade," and reported, "All 118 million shares were preordered, providing an ultimate return of $1.726 billion . . ." Like the mergers of the U.S. railways and the $1.4-billion offering of Falconbridge Ltd. stock that generated $57 million in dealer fees in July, the Petro-Canada triumph signalled the climate was right for the even bigger CN deal.

Dampening the good news, however, was Quebec. On September 7, the Parti Québécois government tabled a referendum bill— "Quebec's Declaration of Independence" that included the question the province's voters would face on October 30: "Do you agree that Quebec should become sovereign, after having made a formal offer to Canada for a new economic and political partnership . . ." If the Yes side won, no one knew what would happen. Canada's survival might be at risk. At the very least, a Yes victory would plunge Canada into the kind of political confusion and economic uncertainty investors hate. Who would buy shares in a transcontinental railway that had to rattle through such a mess?

On September 30, a poll showed the No (keep-Canada-together) voters led the Yes voters by 53.2 per cent to 46.8 per cent. In October the gap kept narrowing until, just two days before the referendum, the same pollsters, Léger and Léger, reported the electorate equally divided at 50-50. The federal government, CN and its underwriters, however, had already decided they had no choice but to barrel ahead with plans to sell the corporation in mid-November.

Throughout October, arguments flew from the mouths of both federalists and sovereigntists. Insults, warnings, bickering and back-biting dominated the media. Minister of Finance Paul Martin told Quebeckers a Yes vote would cost them their passports, currency, seats in the federal Parliament, the 128-year-old economic union and up to a million jobs. Quebec Premier Jacques Parizeau told them a No vote would prompt big business to "spit in our soup" and the federal government to "kick our asses." Bloc Québécois leader Lucien Bouchard, the most eloquent of the sovereigntists, claimed a Yes vote would be "like magic. With a wave of the wand it changes everything."

Enough Quebec voters appeared to believe him that Prime Minister Jean Chrétien—while delivering an urgent, eleventh-hour television speech—sorrowfully pleaded with them to come up with "one good reason to destroy Canada."

Meanwhile, the push to privatize CN continued as though the times were normal. While Quebec leaders were denouncing one another as racists and liars, rail analysts were winding up their investigations of CN.

Rail analysts are sleuths, salespeople and storytellers.

"Yablon goes to Canada," Gary Yablon of Schroder Wertheim, New York, explains. "He looks at CN trains, does an analysis to understand the customers and the earnings potential, writes up a report, goes down the hall to [his] sales force and says, 'We're gonna be an underwriter for this deal. Tell all your clients to buy this for these five reasons.' Maybe a day later, CN management comes here for a meeting with the sales force and tells the story their way. No mistakes allowed [by management], because for the sales guys, the first impression is the most important impression—in spades, in this business.

"Then the salespeople just start hitting the phones, calling the Fidelities of the world, the institutions in the U.S., Canada, overseas. They say, 'We're in this deal, our analyst likes it, he thinks the stock will go from here to there, and here's why you should buy it.'"

While analyzing CN, Yablon interviewed experts on the industries it served. "I have three or four coal sources who deal with international trade, for example," he explains. "I tell them, 'CN says production in this mine over here will grow by two million tons in five years. Do you buy that?' "

Yablon also rides the trains. "But frankly," he acknowledges, "anything nicer than a Lexington Avenue subway feels great to me. I don't look for anything outside of scenery on a train. What I look for in the *numbers* are trends and opportunities in track structure, density and utilization of cars and locomotives, etc. To try and sniff out discrepancies. My job is like an investigator's."

Firing questions at railway staff, he assesses not just what they say, but how they appear while saying it. "You've got to look 'em right in the eye. What's the mood in the yard? Sometimes, numbers tell you only a very small part of the story."

Craig Kloner of Goldman, Sachs says, "One of the things you do is what you call 'high rail.' You get into a little truck that rides along the rails. You get out and inspect the track, the ballasting, the ties, the signalling. You discuss the particular geography with the local superintendent, go through the locomotives and have your locomotive expert inspect the ones that have been rebuilt."

Kloner interviews the railway's customers and examines not only its physical assets, but its balance sheet, cash flow, capital requirements and competitive environment. "All of those things go into our analysis of the current and future value of a railroad," Kloner says, "but most people, all they look at are the reported earnings per share."

"Kloner was a guy whose role in this thing you just can't overestimate," Michael Sabia says. "Talk about going the extra mile. Everywhere we had a meeting, in Europe or the U.S., he'd already been there." Kloner says he served as the busy advance man for the CN road show because, "Although we rely heavily on the sales force, to have a very successful transaction, the analyst who did the work must convince the investing public that that work has indeed been done, and the stock should be purchased."

To conquer Canadian doubts about the market for CN stock across the Atlantic, Kloner visited financial institutions and Goldman,

Sachs sales forces in several European cities. Working from the prospectus and answering the questions it raised among money managers, he told the CN privatization story again and again. Shortly after he returned, during a discussion about CN's impending road show, he advised Canadian bureaucrats that Goldman, Sachs could probably sell *all* the stock in Europe. At that moment, he says, the Canadians knew the transaction would be a hit.

"I also went to major cities in the U.S.," Kloner says. "I talked with the sales forces and all the financial institutions so that they heard [the Initial Public Offering story] not only on the conference call I did with potential buyers, but in face-to-face conversations. By the time I'd gone through Europe and the U.S., perhaps 90 per cent of the stock was sold to people I'd seen."

In May 1994, Kloner had discovered he had cancer. While going the extra mile for the CN privatization in the summer and fall of 1995, he was enduring chemotherapy.

On October 18, the global coordinators set the price range of CN shares at CDN$22.50 to $25.50 (payable in two installments) and promised the privatized railway would issue annual dividends of 80 cents per share. With the price-range announcement, the official marketing effort was off and running. But interest in the IPO was already so high, said Evan Siddall of Nesbitt Burns, that "we had people before we started marketing, before we actually told anybody a single thing about the company. It was fantastic." Even before publication of the price range, the underwriters had begun to build their books.

"When we build a book," Siddall continued, "we're taking orders. People say, 'I want a million shares at this price or at no price. Whatever you can come up with, I want a million.' And we had a lot of those with CN. When they say they'll take so many shares, we have their contract. Our business is done on the basis of oral contracts. When you think about the number of dollars and people involved, it's incredible. It's all done that way. Now we do sign firm contracts after the fact, just to make sure there aren't any screw-ups, but it's understood that if you give us an order for a million shares, and we say you may have a million, then we have a commitment."

While sales forces pitched the IPO by phone, Tellier, Sabia, Jack McBain, senior vice-president, operations, and Gerald Davies, senior vice-president, marketing, hit the road. Accompanying them were James Foote, vice-president, investor relations, Canadian and U.S. bankers, and a team of show-biz technicians from the British-based road-show specialists, Imagination Ltd. Travelling by commercial airlines, private jets and limousines, they visited twenty-six cities in nine nations on two continents and—up to eight times a day, for an hour at a time—delivered the dry news from the prospectus in a crisp, dramatic and entertaining fashion. All in three weeks.

"Before going through this," says fitness buff Tellier, "I could not have imagined one could put one's mind and body through such an exhausting exercise. The human body is just a fantastic machine."

The CN men made their presentations to the sales forces of half-a-dozen investment banks in Toronto and Manhattan just before the road show started in Winnipeg. In their absence, mountains of work arose on their desks. "So it wasn't until about Christmas," Davies remembers, "that we could unwind a bit. We slept a long time. The road show was a draining process. I wouldn't have missed it for anything, but I'm not sure I'd want to do it again."

The show had to have enough pizzazz to grip audiences of the most tough-minded investment professionals in the world—and enough concise, relevant information to persuade them to put tens of millions of dollars into CN. Each presentation exposed the CN performers to the analysts' judgements, just as actors face judgement on an opening night. Since many in the audiences already knew that the right managers could make CN run profitably, what they really wanted to assess, with their own eyes, was whether *these* managers—Tellier, Sabia and company—had the ability and grit to do it. To those who had expressed reservations about two ex-bureaucrats running a Class I railway, Kloner had said, "Wait until you see them. You'll find they're the most unusual bureaucrats you've ever met."

The road show was all about seeing them. The goal was to turn a promising privatization into the best in Canadian history. To whip the performers into shape for the job, CN turned to Imagination Ltd.

Founded in London in 1975 by Paul MacKay, an Australian-born entrepreneur, the firm sells "brand-experience management." It employed 220 people in 1995 and reaped annual revenues of more than £45 million. According to Bernard Leibov, Imagination's project manager for the CN show, the work involves "getting people to *experience* a company," rather than having them merely hear or read about it. The techniques include film, song, dance, the spoken word or whatever else suits the product. Like MacKay, many Imagination staff have theatre backgrounds.

The company started running road shows for corporations in 1986 and had produced sixty-five for clients around the world by the mid-1990s. A former investment banker with Goldman, Sachs who works out of Imagination's Manhattan office, the South African-born Leibov says the company "has done every major privatization in all of Europe."

CN's dealings with Imagination began in May, just as transport minister Doug Young introduced the CN Commercialization Act in the House of Commons. Goldman, Sachs arranged for MacKay and Leibov to meet Tellier, Sabia, Torrance Wylie and Wes Kelley in Montreal. From then until mid-October, Imagination, CN and the underwriters worked together on the road show's script, style and schedule.

The work did not always run smoothly. CN's contribution was, in Leibov's delicate phrase, "unusually significant." Sabia was extremely demanding, and at first Leibov found it hard "to get CN to believe we knew what to do." All Tellier and Sabia could see was him and MacKay, "not the fifteen people in London who'd be working on the production." At one point, Sabia wanted to fire Imagination. Later, he cheerfully acknowledged his mistake and the company's flawless work for CN. "Preparing for the road show, we were all pretty antsy," Sabia explains, "and I was just damned determined this would be the best damned road show in the whole damned world. I was focused—to put it mildly."

"He was tough to work with," Leibov says, "but in the end the product was much better because of him."

Sabia was as tough on himself as he was on Imagination and the underwriters. "There were a lot of financial issues in that prospectus, so I was apprehensive as hell about how the show would go," Sabia says. "I studied for it like I was back studying for an economics exam. I was determined that, on the finance side, there'd never be any question I couldn't answer."

The theatre version of the show, which as many as 800 money managers saw at a crack, started with a four-and-a-half minute video. The film featured dramatic footage of CN in action from coast to coast, surging music and a voice-over that ringingly concluded CN was "heralding a new era in a vital international service." Tellier delivered a punchy speech about the strategies for the CN turnaround and what had already been done to achieve it; McBain described the slashing of costs and improvements in service; Sabia weighed in with a pithy account of the railway's mightily improved financial health; and Tellier returned to the podium to say, "Thank you for being here," give a twenty-second pitch on "a new CN" that would "deliver double-digit earnings" and await a barrage of loaded questions from the floor.

Sharing the stage with Tellier, Sabia and McBain was Gerald Davies, ready to explain the revolution he was leading in CN's marketing. Davies completed what vice-president Foote saw as an all-star cast: "We had Paul, whose political and government background, in this instance, was a positive. It made him the only guy who could have carried this thing through. We had Michael, the supersmart CFO. We had Gerald Davies, this Texas marketer with big railroad connections. We had Jack McBain, the guy that runs your trains, the guy with stability who's been around forever."

They also had Foote himself, who knew the U.S. railway investment community as a small-town mayor knows the only barbershop in town.

Essential to the quality of the show, which the media liked to call "a slick audio-visual presentation," was the computer-based Aston Motif video-graphic system, which produces the maps and other images behind an announcer's head during network news. "The system went everywhere," Leibov says. "There were six pieces of equipment, and the operator carried it all himself, in a heavy metal case." Imagination hired projection and sound equipment in each city, but a rostrum, lectern, desk, chairs, teleprompter and large backdrop accompanied the troupe. The sheer size of Canada and the tightness of the schedule posed a rare problem for Leibov. With back-to-back presentations in Winnipeg, Calgary, Vancouver, Toronto and Montreal, the only way to produce every show on time was to leapfrog identical sets of equipment over cities. "That whole week in Canada was unusual and very satisfying to us," Leibov says.

The show had more modest presentations for smaller audiences, but the information the CN men delivered remained the same. So did the ceaseless pressure never to let up on the intensity of their performance.

They had swallowed some pride while perfecting their act. "I was very reluctant, and so was Sabia, to stick to a script because that's not the way we speak publicly," Tellier says. "I felt I was in a bit of a straitjacket." But to satisfy the audiences, for whom time was not only money but *big* money, and to keep to a schedule that sometimes hustled the performers through three airports in one day, they had to limit each presentation to one hour at the outside. Any ad-libbing would steal time from the next speaker or the question-and-answer period.

If their timing had to be flawless, their oratorical style had to express confidence, ability and drive. Paul MacKay taught them how to use the teleprompter effectively, and Mark Tercek of Goldman, Sachs was among those who coached them on delivery. "We had rehearsals, with the music and everything," Tellier says, "and they'd say, 'You've got to project your energy level. You're a very energetic guy. Well, it has to come out loud and clear. These people are going to watch you for sixty minutes.' Or they'd say, 'You speak too fast, or you don't speak fast enough, or change this, or change that.' In the end, it was a very well-rehearsed presentation."

Saying the same things in the same way several times a day for weeks on end was drudgery, yet the performers had to be "up" for every presentation. "You may have performed extremely well at Sceptre in Toronto at eight in the morning, and at MacKenzie Financial at nine, but when you walk into Beutel Goodman at ten, they don't give a damn how well you did in the previous two hours," Tellier says. "So you perform or you don't perform, and to say you don't perform at ten but you're going to do extremely well at eleven is just not good enough, because by eleven the ten o'clock opportunity is gone forever."

They never knew beforehand how many people they would face or who they would be. Since Tellier was the first speaker, he had to assess each audience quickly. "You read the body language," he says. "It's fascinating. A book on the psychology of these meetings could be written. You have to instantly figure out who you're talking to and what they're interested in, and also be ready to deal with any question without appearing to be taken by surprise.

"The questioners in the U.S were often highly aggressive. I'd tell the CN story with my colleagues, and then somebody would shout, 'Who are you? What have you done in your life?' Very personal questions. 'How long are you going to stick around in this job? You made some changes at the top, but you didn't change everybody on the payroll, so what makes you think you can change the corporate culture? How much money are *you* investing in this company?' And you can't go out of there saying, 'Gee, you know, I wish I'd answered this and this to that question.' "

Tellier had a fast answer on his personal stake in the CN of the future. He had already borrowed $400,000 to buy shares. Indeed, he and his colleagues came up with the right answers to just about all the questions fired at them.

Looking back, Kloner praised the CN team for "the willingness to go through an agonizing process, to work diligently—and often to endure a pain in the ass from Goldman, Sachs, who pushed them to work diligently—on the structure and content of that show until, right out of a box, they could perform it in an extraordinarily convincing fashion. They did one of the most professional jobs on a road show that I have ever seen in my life."

Canada Survives,
Road Show Rolls On

They called her their "guardian angel." Sarah Brennan of Surrey, England, the logistics manager from Imagination, booked hotels, flights and limousines for the CN road-show players, arranged all their creature comforts and set up rooms and halls for their performances. Brennan was on the go by six every morning. She registered the troupe at hotels, met them at airports with their keys in hand and , even when they failed to reach their rooms till nearly midnight, made sure their shirts were laundered and their suits pressed by dawn. Bernard Leibov calls her "just an amazing manager." The bills from Imagination eventually surpassed $2.27 million, but Brennan was one of many reasons the price was right. Paul Tellier had high praise for Imagination's entire road-show team, including the technicians.

On Monday, October 30, 1995, the CN executives attended

morning meetings with three financial institutions in Paris, made a presentation over lunch at Hotel Le Bristol, flew to Milan by private jet, gave another presentation, with cocktails, in a hall on Piazza Della Repubblica and, again by private jet, flew to Zurich. At 10:30 P.M., they found themselves in the heart of this rich Swiss city, long renowned for financial institutions.

They stayed overnight at the Widder, a medium-sized hotel of rare character and grace in which no two rooms are alike. Tellier and Michael Sabia, however, were in no mood to savour its charms. Tellier had learned that at three in the morning—nine at night, Montreal time—a French television network would transmit to Zurich live coverage of the referendum vote in Quebec. He phoned Sabia about the show, set his alarm for three and went to bed. When he arose, the sovereigntists were beating the federalists by an alarming margin. He watched the coverage for three nail-biting hours. Dawn was breaking over the River Limmat in Zurich when, across the Atlantic Ocean, the federalists squeaked through to a razor-thin victory. The vote was 50.6 per cent No to 49.4 per cent Yes.

"By then, I was too hyper to stay in bed," Tellier says. "I got up and went running for half an hour. And I took a shower."

Sabia had been sick to his stomach in Paris and was still feeling shaky. "But I couldn't sleep that night in Zurich because the vote was so close," he recalls. "I was thinking so, okay, what happens tomorrow morning? If the good guys lose, what do we do? I was thinking through a game plan so that if Paul and I had to sit down in the morning, I wanted that laid out: steps A, B, C, D and E. So I was working on that, in case the worst happened."

By 8 A.M., at Hauz zum Ruden, in a beautiful, third-floor room overlooking the river, the CN men were performing for representatives of some twenty Swiss financial institutions.

"Mr. Tellier," a woman asked, "what about the Quebec situation?"

"Well, there was a referendum yesterday," he replied, "and we won."

"Yes, I know," she joked, "by eleven votes."

At 11:05 A.M. that same day, October 31, the team flew to Frankfurt by private jet to make presentations, and by 6 P.M. reached Rotterdam for a meeting. They then drove to Amsterdam and, though they didn't arrive at the Amstel Inter-Continental till 10 P.M., chose to spend a rare boys' night out. Tellier went to work in his room, but the other CN men, along with a couple of the North American bankers and some Imagination staff, had a jovial dinner at a canal-side French restaurant, Le Quatre Canetons.

Since the road show had started back in Winnipeg, an *esprit de corps* had been growing among the players. In the airplanes and limousines, Jack McBain endured ribbings about his style publicly touting the BELTPACK. The men rated one another's latest performances on a score of one to ten. "Over dinner, after a long day," Evan Siddall says, "we'd start imitating each other. It was very funny, and that night in Amsterdam, in a constructive way, we were all taking swings at each other and making fun of each other." They would all remember that dinner, far from home on Halloween night.

"We knew we were in the middle of just a horrendous week," McBain says, "and yet to have that chance to sit back and have a few laughs was tremendous."

"In retrospect, it was a turning point," Sabia adds. "The last hurdle had been cleared. The referendum was over. It was close, but we won. The road show would continue and from now on, it's just blow the lights out. We hadn't been doing badly before, but now there was really a significant step up in our level of performance."

After meetings in Amsterdam and Edinburgh on Wednesday, November 1, they spent a long, hard Thursday in London. It was there that Sabia showed his new confidence. At a small gathering in London, he banged a tabletop with his fist while telling a particularly annoying skeptic that the fellow didn't know what he was talking about. "Let me tell you how this is going to be," Sabia said. The Initial Public Offering would be a huge success, "and if you want to buy the stock, that's fine." If he didn't, that was fine, too.

The atmosphere in Boston and New York, where in mid-November the road show faced its most critical and important crowds, was intensely competitive. Several other major shows, including one for Victoria's Secret lingerie, were performing for the same investors and money managers that CN was wooing.

"The team from Victoria's Secret considered gaining attention by sending a model, wearing the company's merchandise, down to the trading floor of the New York Stock Exchange," Tellier says, "but we decided sending Jack McBain down in his engineers' overalls just wouldn't draw the same response. We stuck to the basics."

By then, the CN show had become precise, rhythmic and dynamic. Even before a CN performer could call out the number of a slide to illustrate the answer to a question from the floor, Imagination technicians smoothly projected the right one. The performers knew they were on a roll, the roll of their lives. "We were almost sort of high-fiving at the end of each meeting," Sabia says. "I mean, we were just goin' at it."

The IPO would have succeeded in any event, but the Goldman, Sachs men believe it was the power and professionalism of the road show that turned the offering into a smash hit.

In addition to the show for investors, the corporation, with the help of Wertheim and Co. Inc., Toronto, and Towers Perrin, Montreal, ran road shows for CN employees in French and English. The shows were part of perhaps the biggest work-force education program the corporation had ever undertaken. Although CN could not twist employees' arms to make them buy shares in the company, it gave them a booklet, *Before You Invest*, on the principles of stock-market investing; instructions and forms for ordering CN shares; information, including a letter from Tellier, on the direction in which CN was heading; and a 1-800 number whose operators had the answers to all questions about the share offering.

Staff morale was crucially important to CN's future, yet many union members saw the job-slashing of the previous three years and the back-to-work legislation of mid-June as bitter defeats. News of more work-force reductions was in the air. To calm the fears, assure employees about the future of a newly efficient and privatized CN, and arouse their interest in the Employee Share Participation Plan, the corporation—having trained thirty-eight of its own staff as "communicators"—sponsored 314 "information sessions." These occurred right across Canada and were attended by 6,599 employees.

Many of the presentations featured both a video that showed Tellier and Sabia delivering a version of their presentations for the international road show, and a pitch about the plan that enabled employees to buy up to $4000 worth of CN stock at the public offering price and then automatically receive further shares as a bonus.

Union leaders predicted few of their members would invest in a railway that had treated them so harshly, but in the end, no fewer than 11,080 CN employees invested in the shares. That was more than 42 per cent of CN's total payroll, the highest proportion of employee ownership of any railway in North America. Their average investment was $2,234.

By early November, when the CN team of executives headed back across the Atlantic, everyone but the most hidebound investors and business columnists knew the demand for CN shares would be extraordinary. The low expectations of the past had actually worked in CN's favour. The more inefficient CN had once been, the more room there had been for improvement, and the greater the improvement to be achieved, the greater the opportunity for profit. American investors generally understood this better than Canadians.

But there was another reason why Sabia called CN's poor reputation "one of the great aces up our sleeve." If you think you're going to meet Bill Gates, and you meet one of his vice-presidents, you're disappointed. "But the opposite happens, too," Sabia says. "You can be pleasantly surprised. People said, 'This is CN, and it's trying to get investors to buy it? Come on, they're just a bunch of stumblebum bureaucrats who can't manage their way out of a paper bag.' But then they discover we have a *plan*, we're carrying it through and we know what we're doing."

On November 8, nine days before the CN shares traded on stock markets for the first time, John Embry, a vice-president at Royal Bank Investment Management Inc., marvelled, "Quite frankly, I was amazed when they came to see us [during the road show]. You have this impression of the nation's railroad as a bunch of dunderheads, but they were really quite impressive. They had a game plan and were sort of modelling themselves after U.S. railroads."

Demand was galloping so fast, the *Globe and Mail* reported, that "some buyers are actually padding their orders, asking for more than they expect to get in the largest privatization in Canadian history." Underwriters, Embry said, had told him, " 'You are going to get huge cutbacks, so if you want a certain amount of stock, you'd better pad the order.' I would be shocked if this didn't sell out."

As the demand increased till the shares were at least eight times oversubscribed, a fight erupted between Goldman, Sachs and the Canadian bankers. The government and CN had led Goldman, Sachs to believe that, in the initial allocation of shares, roughly half would go to the foreign underwriters ("foreign" mostly meant American) and half to the Canadians. Suddenly faced with an enormous demand by favoured clients at mutual and pension funds, however, the Canadians now insisted on taking the lion's share, perhaps 70 per cent. In underwriters' fees, millions of dollars were at stake.

Lined up behind the lead Canadian underwriters, ScotiaMcLeod and Nesbitt Burns, were the brokerages to which they were farming out some of the business. This syndicate included the investment arms of Canada's biggest chartered banks, and the major independent houses. Goldman, Sachs's closest allies were Morgan Stanley & Co. Inc., J. P. Morgan Securities Inc., and Schroder Wertheim & Co. Inc.

The Goldman, Sachs case went like this:

First, it was on the basis of Canada's *promise* of 50 per cent for the foreign underwriters that Goldman, Sachs asked international investors to work hard to learn the CN story and assured them they would get their fair share of the stock.

Second, Goldman, Sachs did its job so well it could have sold all the stock by itself. It boasted what partner John Downing calls "a very impressive book." He says, "I believed in the merit of that book, in the quality of the demand we had produced." U.S. financial institutions had put between US$50 billion and $60 billion into railways. "They understood CN," Downing continues. "They knew what they had here, and *we* knew they'd pay a high price on the deal in the aftermarket, a price certainly well above what the Canadian institutions would pay."

Third, Goldman, Sachs's strategic advice, experience with railway share offerings, knowledge of the U.S. industry, superior sales force and general clout had made the IPO the success it was turning out to be, not the Canadian bankers. "It was not until we had made it perfectly clear that this was going to be a highly successful transaction that the Canadian investment banks suddenly realized they had a hot deal on their hands," Craig Kloner says. As the campaign to cut back the foreigners' share peaked, he adds, "Let's just say my level of irritation was fairly high."

Although the Canadian underwriters certainly persuaded institutions in Canada to buy CN shares, no one in the railway or government doubted that, among the banks, the real force driving the IPO towards its unprecedented triumph was Goldman, Sachs. Even months before the IPO, the decision to ask a New York bank to participate in the deal had intrigued Canadians because, as finance minister Paul Martin says, "We don't pay any attention to something unless the Americans have said they're interested in it."

The Canadian bankers, for their part, believed CN and the government should never have been so foolish as to promise the foreigners 50 per cent. They insisted they deserved as much as 70 per cent of the shares because CN was *Canadian* and because Canadian taxpayers had sunk billions into it.

"We needed the Americans," Gordon Lackenbauer of Nesbitt Burns acknowledges. "We needed both their money and their expertise. We could never have pulled it off without the U.S. But here was this big pig that Canadians had subsidized for generations, and you're finally pulling off a superb privatization, and you're letting the Americans come right in and walk off with a billion-dollar chunk of it. In our view, if they wanted it that badly, well, let them go for it in the aftermarket in Canada and drive up the price."

The angry showdown, a meeting nobody would remember with pleasure, occurred on Saturday afternoon, November 11. That was one day before the road show moved on to New York, five days before the government sold CN to the underwriters and six days before the shares began to trade on stock markets. As a convenience to transport minister Doug Young, bound for China on government business, the antagonists met at the Montreal Aéroport Hilton. Young and Martin sat at one end of a table, Tellier at the other. CN Chairman David McLean was there, as well as Sabia, David Dodge from finance, Moya Green from Transport Canada, and two bankers from each of Nesbitt Burns, ScotiaMcLeod and Goldman, Sachs.

One purpose of the meeting was to discuss a new price range. "David Dodge played a key role in the pricing," Sabia says. "His perspective was that you couldn't get 100 per cent sold at one blow if it was too aggressively priced, that it was crucially important for the government to send a message to the international market that Canada could do these things right, and that this mattered more than fifty cents on the price. His intervention was critical."

Out of the meeting came a decision to move the price range up to between $25.50 per share and $27.50, which would still offer investors a premium of 35 per cent over the stock of comparable U.S. railways.

With respect to the allocation, McLean had advised Tellier and Sabia that the 50-50 division was politically tricky for the government, yet they remained in the Goldman, Sachs camp. "The Wall Street mystique was persuasive," says David Wilson of Scotia-McLeod. "CN and the government were somewhat cowed by big, powerful firms from Wall Street."

Tellier argued, first, that CN, on the government's behalf, had been telling investors all over Europe and the U.S. that the allocation would be 50-50, and that Canada should keep its word. Second, to keep CN on its toes during its race to become a first-class railway, it needed among its shareholders a major proportion of railway-smart Americans. Third, having foreigners invest in Canada in a big way, despite the referendum frenzy, was a vote of confidence in the country. Finally, it was good for Canada to show, for the first time, that it could raise a huge amount of money from U.S. markets.

The American and Canadian underwriters vehemently defended their positions. Remembering the afternoon a year later, Lackenbauer said, "That was the roughest meeting I've ever been at." Wilson of ScotiaMcLeod called it "a classic high-drama meeting." One Canadian banker acknowledged that a certain amount of greed lay behind the Canadian case, but insisted "the Wall Street bullies were motivated by *pure* greed. Their anger was driven by greed alone."

"At one point," Tellier recalls, "I said to one of the Canadian brokers, 'Would you please put your greed aside for a moment and just think about the good of the Canadian government, which is trying to sell this railroad.' He didn't like that much."

"This is what was quite stressful," Young says. "First of all, I was, as Hubert Humphrey said, as pleased as punch they'd pulled it off. We were within minutes of putting it to bed, the biggest deal in Canadian history. And then, at the last minute, to become aware that these guys are really upset because they're not making a few million dollars *more* for themselves—and my pay is $124,000 a year. Well, I didn't have a whole lot of sympathy."

Sabia regarded the squabble as a sign of success. CN had deliberately fostered "demand tension" among the underwriters and should not have been surprised that it resulted in some tough talk. "So there was greed on the American side, and rightly so, and there was greed on the Canadian side, and rightly so," he says. "That's the whole idea. For a deal like this to succeed, you have to harness greed, and, yes, it got pretty tense."

Martin and Young briefly withdrew from the meeting. When they returned, Martin announced the government's ruling: Forty per cent of the shares would go to the institutional market in the U.S., 40 per cent would go to the institutional market in Canada and the Canadian retail market would get the other 20 per cent. This decision cost American banks about CDN$8 million in fees.

"So you've done all that work, and you get to the final opportunity to be rewarded for what you've done," Downing says, "and you walk in with one of the highest-quality books of institutional demand we've ever had—and you get tooled around for political reasons. It was not unexpected, but it was frustrating."

"The importance of the financial industry *per se* has grown, along with a phenomenal increase in international capital flow," Martin explains. "In many ways, financial businesses today are what the railroads once were, and it's important under these circumstances to encourage the Canadian dealers. But the second thing, which was very important, was that this was an asset that had been paid for by Canadian taxpayers, and it was perfectly reasonable that Canadian taxpayers be given a disproportionate share of the ownership. If they chose to dispose of it later, that was their business. But, at least, I thought it was our responsibility to recognize generations of Canadian ownership."

They Couldn't Get Enough

I n the two months before the Initial Public Offering, at least two dozen people were attending the privatization meetings at CN headquarters. They included CN executives, auditors, lawyers, bureaucrats, bankers and consultants. "Everybody had to know what everybody else was doing," says Claude Mongeau, vice-president, strategic and financial planning. "And you had to put all these different things together so that everybody was feeling happy enough to give their sign-off letters. The last few weeks, it was like bringing home some huge boat."

Late on November 16, 1995, the underwriters and government agreed on the final price: $27 per share. The deal was done. The closing date would be November 28, but the price agreement meant the underwriters had effectively bought CN. That same night, assorted lawyers gathered at Quebecor Printing in downtown Montreal to doctor the final prospectus. A deadline loomed. If they failed to deliver the document to the appropriate securities commissions on time, there'd be no trading of CN shares when the markets opened at 9:30 the next morning.

Wrangling over wording at the print shop were auditors, lawyers for auditors, Canadian and American lawyers for CN, Canadian and American lawyers for the government, and Canadian and American lawyers for the banks. Since CN's top managers were on the last leg of the road show, Mongeau says, "I was holding the fort." In his memory, some twenty-five lawyers bickered all night in the Quebecor building. "I remember the government lawyers and our own counsel, they were still arguing at five in the morning," he says. "There were almost fistfights."

He escaped at 5.30 A.M., and little more than three hours later joined Michael Sabia on the trading floor of Goldman, Sachs in Lower Manhattan. Sabia, too, was so exhausted he felt like falling down. The day was Friday, November 17. He'd been on the road show in New York on Monday and Tuesday and in Boston on Wednesday. He'd gone back to New York "to see the book" at Goldman, Sachs on Thursday morning, returned to Montreal that same day "to resolve a whole bunch of little last-minute things." Now, Friday morning, here he was again at Goldman, Sachs.

During the dank, chilly Montreal spring of 1995, Sabia and Mongeau had talked about some day seeing the lit-up initials of CN on stock-market tickers. Now, after nine months of the hardest work of their lives, after blow-ups, plots and confrontations, they stood together in the Goldman, Sachs capital markets trading room. With them was Craig Kloner, whom Sabia says "almost killed himself making this deal work."

As the opening of the New York Stock Exchange approached, the excitement grew. They were on the fiftieth floor of New York Plaza in Lower Manhattan. Beyond the big windows was New York harbour, Ellis Island and the Statue of Liberty. "Jeez," Sabia recalls, "it was like in *Bonfire of the Vanities*. There was this sea of trading desks. People were rushing up to congratulate us. One guy had a big stack of CN orders at his elbow, and he was talking and yelling and dealing on the phone. It was just like a movie."

The ticker-tape symbol for the stock in New York was CNIPP, the I to distinguish it from another CN, the Ps signifying Partial Payment for a first installment. "That was a very moving moment," Sabia says, remembering the sight of CNIPP moving on the ticker for the very first time. "I'll never forget it."

"The federal government . . . pulled off the biggest initial public offering in the country's history," the *Globe and Mail* reported, "selling Canadian National Railways for $2.2 billion, or $27 a share, to investors clamoring to get on board. CN's initial public offering of 76.2 million shares, plus an extra provision of 7.6 million, was sold out well in advance of last night's final pricing."

According to the official count, the government raised CDN$2.16 billion by selling 83,800,000 common shares of CN to underwriting syndicates. Although the price was $27 per share, investors paid only $16.25 on closing, with the second installment payment, $10.75, due on November 26, 1996.

Much of the action Sabia and Mongeau were watching was Canadians taking quick profits as they sold CN to Americans.

"Michael knew, Paul Martin knew, and certainly Paul Tellier knew, that the 60 per cent of the shares placed in Canada would stay there for about twenty minutes," John Downing of Goldman, Sachs says. The Americans still had a stronger faith in CN's future than the Canadians, and were therefore willing to pay a higher price for the shares. Much of the 20 per cent that Martin had insisted go to the Canadian retail market began to flood south within minutes of the stock exchanges' opening on that first day of trading, and many of the shares Canadian institutions had bought soon followed them. Within days, the ownership of CN switched from being 60-40 in favour of the Canadians to 60-40 for the foreigners. Within weeks, it was 65-35 for the foreigners. The market had spoken.

Next to the days on which he was married and his son was born, Evan Siddall of Nesbitt Burns called November 17, 1995, the most exciting day of his life. He went to the firm's new, $30-million trading room half an hour before the markets opened. "Our traders were already hammering away," he recalled, "showing where they were prepared to buy and sell the CN stock. There was a swell building up in the market: $18, $18.10, $18.20 . . . At first the drive increments were slow, but in the last few minutes the opening price was just rocketing up. It was incredibly exciting. Our head trader was raising the price as fast as he could talk."

The head trader's job took extraordinary powers of concentration. "He's not only being screamed at by his own salespeople and other traders who are working for him trading the stock," Siddall continued, "he's also hearing from our London office over a speaker, from our New York office over a speaker, from Montreal, from everywhere we have a trading desk. They're all shouting at him, and he's making split-second decisions to either increase or decrease the price. In CN's case, that morning they were just about all increases. So he's trying to organize in his mind—you know, ten, twenty, thirty conversations at any one second."

Most of the analysts the press interviewed predicted that when the markets closed on that first day of trading, the price for the first installment would have risen by one, or at best two dollars above the $16.25 in the IPO. Instead the stock was so hot the installment receipts, listed as CNIR on the Toronto and Montreal exchanges, *opened* at $19.50. In the first five minutes of trading, 8 million shares changed hands.

For a short time after the exchanges opened, Goldman, Sachs failed to strike a balance between the buying and selling prices. That meant Nesbitt Burns, which was running the Canadian syndicate, had a brief but thrilling monopoly on the trading. "American institutions, U.K. institutions, French institutions, Canadian institutions—they were all pushing their trade through Toronto," Siddall said. "So all the volume flowed through the Nesbitt Burns desk. The activity was frantic. It was absolutely incredible."

"The demand for Canadian National Railways shares swept the Canadian and U.S. stock markets like wildfire yesterday as traders burned up the phones trying to fill orders," the *Globe and Mail* reported on November 18. After a frenzied day of trading, the stock closed at $20.25.

Downing had won a wager. At the meeting to set the final price for the IPO, when some Canadians wondered if $27 wasn't too high, he had bet Kenneth Copland of Nesbitt Burns that, within one month, the price of the first installment receipt would rise high enough so that a year later, when investors paid $10.25 for the second installment, the price would be not $27 but $30. Since the $16.25 rose by an unprecedented $4 on November 17, Downing won his bet in just one day. Copland happily paid him, but to remind him of the allocation battle of the week before, wrote him cheques for $60 in Canadian and $40 in U.S. currency.

In the *Financial Post*, columnist William Hanley playfully assessed what November 17 meant to the "Bay Streeters" who had recently suffered big cuts in their bonuses: "As the messages of sympathy and support were pouring in from across a grieving nation, the CN gravy train pulled into the Toronto Stock Exchange and the Street clambered thankfully aboard. With more than 28 million receipts traded at $4 above the $16.25 price of the first installment, this meant needed millions would supplement the meagre tens of millions in fees from those tightwads in Ottawa. There is justice and fairness in the world after all. Even on Bay Street."

Fred Ketchen of ScotiaMcLeod marvelled, "I can't remember any [initial offering] coming to market in Canada—either a corporate or a government issue—at that kind of price, and seeing it jump more than three dollars on the first day."

"It's unheard of for a Canadian stock to trade that way," said Aldo Sunseri of BPI Capital, Toronto.

"Certainly we're happy, and a bit dazzled by the volume and price," Gordon Lackenbauer said. "We never really expected this to happen. It must have built up such a head of steam it couldn't stop."

The deal, he added, was "a model of how a company should be privatized."

On the morning Sabia and Siddall experienced exhilaration in trading rooms in Manhattan and Toronto, Tellier went to work at CN headquarters in Montreal. Using the public address system for the first time, he told every employee in the building that this day was the first page in a new chapter of the CN story. He held a brief meeting with his vice-presidents and spoke to 200 CN executives across the country on a conference call.

He had ended his major road-show presentations by vowing, "We are determined to ensure this progress continues. We are determined to continue to downsize. We are determined to increase asset utilization. We are determined to ensure this is an investor-driven company. We are determined to deliver, and I am confident we will." Privatization, he said, was not an end in itself, but simply a way to institutionalize change.

Every weekday morning from now on, Tellier would see the big stock ticker in the CN lobby. Showing the minute-by-minute price of CN shares in bold, red letters, it would silently score the performance of him and his staff and remind them of the shareholders they now served.

Like other victories, the CN privatization had many fathers, but vice-president Wes Kelley, who has worked for the railway long enough to have known six presidents, including Donald Gordon, a boss of legendary toughness, says, "Not one of the others could have pulled this off the way Paul Tellier did."

Afterword:
The Best Year Ever

"**F**or the first time in more than 70 years," Mark Hallman reported in the *Financial Post* in late 1995, "Canada has two investor-owned transcontinental national railways."

Just three days after the furious stock-market trading in CN shares began, Canadian Pacific announced it would eliminate 1,450 white-collar jobs and write down $700 million at CP Rail System. Since 80 per cent of the railway's business was in western Canada, it would move its headquarters from Montreal to Calgary. CP Rail would also establish an operating unit to tackle the losses its eastern network incurred. Not only that, but CP Ltd., the conglomerate, would convert CP Rail from a division into a wholly owned subsidiary. This would give the railway its own access to capital markets and increase its flexibility with respect to joint ventures or mergers.

"This is the way it's supposed to be," said business reporter Deirdre McMurdy on CTV's *Canada A.M.* "With a rival railway now on track, aggressively vying for investor capital and market share, Canadian Pacific has at last restructured its rail operation . . . CN's passage from public to private hands has focused both sides on improving their performance, and that's precisely why privatization and deregulation are exceedingly beneficial . . ."

While CN's operating ratio was dropping, so was CP's.

"What's happening is exactly what you'd expect, what any Economics 101 course would tell you," Michael Sabia comments. "Now that we're a much stronger competitor, with a much better cost base than we had, what are they doing? They're working to keep pace."

The flood of CN shares that flashed south on November 17, 1995, occurred because Canadian investors, despite the power of the road show, remained skeptical about Tellier's management team and blind to the railway's long-term promise. Better to grab a big, fast profit, they reasoned, than retain what might be a dog stock, over-priced by excessive promotion.

After that phenomenal first day of trading, a business columnist for Southam News wondered if "the manufactured excitement" over the Initial Public Offering didn't contain "a tad too much reliance on a belief in magic." The rule that no shareholder could own more than 15 per cent of the stock might leave management "beholden to no one, entrenched as it were." Moreover, Paul Tellier was "a political appointee, and this—coupled with the rule that CN must maintain its head office in Montreal—casts an unwanted political shadow on the privatization effort."

The *Globe and Mail*, whose business columnists had been among the IPO's fiercest critics, now suggested the excitement the new shares were arousing was unjustified: " 'What has CN done in Canada,' an investor asked a reporter recently, 'other than to lose money?' Indeed, most Canadians find it hard to imagine CN as a money-making organization . . . Investors may have reason to lose their confidence after the adrenalin rush wears off . . . It may be a long time before CN's shares bear any relation to the company's value . . ."

The Canadian pessimism and suspicion caused some journalists to offer the worst possible investment advice.

On the morning of November 17, even as the price of the CN installment receipts soared, a columnist at the Halifax *Daily News* pooh-poohed the underwriters' claims that the stock was oversubscribed, warning, "The hype says jump on the bandwagon and buy CN shares today, but there's more than a few sharp investors out there who think the issue will be overpriced, and not likely to grow much in the early privatized going. *Caveat emptor*, Cookie."

That same morning, a business reporter for *Canada A.M.* cautioned, "When the market decides to stampede in a certain direction, you can join in or you can get trampled to death, but mark these words: The tide will turn and with a vengeance . . . After all, the buzz was equally excited about the privatization of Air Canada and Petro-Canada. When they were sold to the public, the word was that they were in fighting trim . . . but despite that, there were still lots of nasty surprises for investors . . ."

Such predictions, like those of the previous summer in the Canadian media, would prove to be spectacularly wrong. Stock-market tides have certainly been known to turn with a vengeance, but the price of a CN share, set at $27 on November 16, 1995, rose in less than thirteen months to $57. Many analysts believed it would keep right on climbing till it reached $75 or $80. So much for *caveat emptor*.

Among the Canadian publications whose reporters understood what was really happening at CN was the *Financial Post*, and as 1995 ended, it named Tellier its "overwhelming choice" as Newsmaker of the Year. "Paul Tellier made CN smaller, leaner and more profitable," the *Financial Post* said. "Then he took it to the stock market. Now he's getting on with making CN North America's best railroad." In mid-1996, the Association of American Railroads, the

Regional Railroad Association and the Eastern General Managers Association gave Tellier its Right Hand Man Award; as the year ended, CN's performance had so impressed *Railway Age* that it named him Railroader of the Year.

The corporation had charged into 1996 with its morale high. The road show had instilled a sense of camaraderie in senior management, and for the workers who had survived the job slashing, the privatization was painless. "Tellier had already achieved the painful part," says vice-president Wes Kelley. "No new owners were coming in with brooms for clean sweeps. The shippers wouldn't lose anything. All the tough parts had been done beforehand. There were no losers. It was a happy story."

Throughout CN, a competitive spirit took hold. Workers seemed proud to serve not a government bureaucracy, but a customer-driven, investor-driven railway. The privatization, Tellier says, had been "a tremendously powerful instrument in our transformation. Our people have become a lot more bottom-line oriented. They want to see a higher share price and our performance improve." In short, the revolution in CN's corporate culture was well underway. Its rewards would soon prove dramatic.

For the first time, however, CN management had to answer to a variety of aggressive investors. "At first, we had no adequate systems to satisfy the U.S. market," Sabia says, "and it's data-crazy on railroads. I mean it's ridiculous. So the systems all had to be built." He and his colleagues James Foote and Claude Mongeau did the building.

Speaking of the new kind of pressure CN now endured, Sabia continues, "When you're dealing with a well-informed, highly expert and demanding investor base, sure, every decision counts." He had to balance the long-term interests of CN against the knowledge that investors in such a new company would not tolerate disappointments. "So there's a constant line we walk," he says. "I think we're okay [in the fall of 1996], but I'll tell you, there were moments this year when I said to Jim [Foote, vice-president, investor relations at the time], and Jim and I kid about this a lot, 'Boy, this privatization sounds good when you say it fast, but it certainly narrows one's scope.' You know, it's tricky."

"Mr. Tellier carefully courts the U.S. market, the home of most of CN's big owners and the key analysts," Douglas Goold reported in the *Globe and Mail* in November 1996. "This week, for example, he spent 90 minutes with Scudder Stevens and attended a Salomon Brothers transportation conference. In his view, for a Canadian-based company to succeed in the U.S. market, it must be shareholder-driven and must give analysts the information they want. It helps to be listed on the New York Stock Exchange, as CN was 'from day one.' "

"When we show quarterly results, the first call we make is New York," Tellier says, "and we position ourselves right there with the other railways."

While CN's relentless slashing of costs continued, the corporation now confronted the even tougher challenge of increasing revenue. "The railway industry is generally perceived as *very* mature," said one of CN's own vice-presidents in late 1996. "It is not likely—it is virtually impossible, in fact—that CN can increase its revenue by anything significant. It would take a miracle to increase it by 5 per cent a year over the next ten years." However, CN had no choice but to try to lure business away from truckers, CP and U.S. railways, as well as to open new markets.

"I wasn't a director very long," Purdy Crawford recalled one year after the IPO, "when we started to talk to Paul about shifting his emphasis towards driving the revenue line. And the analysts were saying, 'Okay, Mr. Tellier, how about the top line?' The slogan now is: 'A Billion of Operating Profit by the Year 2000.' "

"The lessons I draw from the rail renewal in the U.S.," Tellier said right after the closing of the IPO, "are that the most successful railroads started, first, to control costs; next phase, improve service; and, three, grow the top line."

Despite two strikes in the auto industry, an unusually long and harsh winter, and what Tellier called "an awful year" for grain, CN's operating profit in 1996 soared to $610 million. Never before had it been so high. It surpassed the figure for 1992, the year Tellier arrived at the railway, by nearly $500 million.

CN's fresh leanness and aggressiveness combined with the variety and balance of its freight to give it a banner year. The new tunnel under the St. Clair River was enabling the corporation to increase its intermodal services faster than those of any other major North American railway. The company's intermodal volume rose 14 per cent in 1996 and 17 per cent in the last quarter. That final quarter also saw a 17 per cent rise in CN revenues from traffic in coal, sulphur and fertilizer, and an 18 per cent growth in its shipments of agricultural products.

Total revenues rose 1.5 per cent to $4.2 billion. Operating expenses dropped by $109 million to $3.5 billion. While CN's profit from continuing operations hit $505 million, special charges of $381 million reduced this to $124 million. Since the chief purpose of the charges was to cover the cost of eliminating 2,250 jobs, the benefits would show up in future balance sheets.

The drop in expenses and rise in revenues caused a decline in CN's operating ratio from 89.3 per cent in 1995 to 85.3 per cent, actually lower than the 1996 target of 85.6 per cent. Under Tellier's leadership, CN had cut its operating ratio by very nearly twelve points since 1992. No other major railway on the continent could match this record of improvement. Moreover, in the final quarter of 1996, as opposed to the full year, CN's operating ratio sank to 80.7 per cent, which rivalled the performance of American carriers.

"We are closing the gap with U.S. railroads," Tellier says. "I won't pretend we can produce every quarter at that level, but our trend line is a good one."

The fourth quarter was exceptional in other respects as well. Under the headline "Newly Private CN Makes Good," the *Journal of Commerce* reported in January 1997, "Canadian National, a private company for less than 15 months, has matched profitability levels that some U.S. railroads have been enjoying in a free-market rail environment since 1980. The railroad posted a fourth-quarter operating income of 208 million Canadian dollars . . ."

For the year as a whole, CN either met, or did better than meet, every target it had set. For the first time ever, it broke even on its eastern operations. It fulfilled all the commitments it had made to potential investors during the road show. "Our credibility was at stake," Tellier says. "It was very important to beat our targets, and we did that."

The *Globe and Mail* at last acknowledged that CN was "truly leaving behind its reputation for bloated inefficiency." "It's one of the most impressive turnarounds I have seen," said Jim Valentine of Salomon Brothers Inc., a giant among New York investment banks. "Mr. Tellier has not been conditioned by traditional railroad thinking."

But even as the compliments flowed in, Tellier was cranking up the pressure on his people to perform. With the work force reduced from 36,000 in 1992 to 21,600, and only 1,250 more jobs to be eliminated, the worst of the downsizing was over. CN was now moving more freight with fewer workers than ever before, but Tellier believed 1997 would be a pivotal year in the CN story and no time for CN employees to relax and pat themselves on the back.

Megamergers among already-huge U.S. railways are making the competition ever stronger and more efficient. "The bar," he says "is continuously raised." The target for the operating ratio in 1997 had been 84.4 per cent; now it would be 83 per cent. The target for 2000 had been 82 per cent; now it would be "below 80 percent."

Early in 1997, Tellier proudly declared that CN's first full year as a privatized company was "the best ever" in the seventy-seven-year history of the company. While the statement made headlines from coast to coast, he was already prodding his more than 21,000 employees to act on his conviction that the best yet simply wasn't good enough.

Sources and
Acknowledgments

To get a grip on this story, I spent weeks sorting through hundreds of newspaper editorials, stories and columns. The articles dated from the mid-1980s to early 1997, and many of the quotes in the book come from them. The *Financial Post* and the *Globe and Mail*'s Report on Business were particularly useful, but I also relied on coverage by the *Vancouver Sun*, Vancouver *Province*, *Calgary Herald*, *Edmonton Journal*, *Winnipeg Free Press*, *Toronto Star*, *Ottawa Citizen*, Montreal *Gazette*, Saint John *Telegraph-Journal*, Halifax *Chronicle-Herald*, *Wall Street Journal*, *Journal of Commerce*, Canadian Press, Southam News, Dow Jones News Service and Knight-Ridder/Tribune Financial News.

I used transcripts of commentaries about CN's privatization from CBC-TV's *Newsworld*, *The National* and CBC Radio's *Morningside*; from CTV's *Canada A.M.*; and from various radio stations across the country. Speeches by CN's Chairman David McLean, President and Chief Executive Officer Paul Tellier, and Senior Vice-President and Chief Financial Officer Michael Sabia gave me important insights into the passion and strategy behind the privatization campaign. Most of the newspaper articles and the speeches came from the fat, loose-leaf binders of Gail Dever. Dever is the director of research and planning at CN's department of public affairs and advertising, and she's a whiz at her job.

I also used magazine articles from *Maclean's, L'Actualité, Canadian Business, Financial World, Montreal Business Magazine, The Economist, Indian Railways, Railway Gazette International, Railway Age, Progressive Railroading* and *Traffic World.* Carol Paterson of CN's library found the railway trade magazines, and that wasn't all she did for me. She dug out academic papers on the U.S. Staggers Act; speeches by past CN presidents; "Railway Financial Viability," a report by the IBI Group for the National Transportation Act Review Commission in 1992; "Railway Financial Viability: The Challenges of Becoming More Competitive," a subsequent study by the IBI Group, commissioned by CP and CN rail systems, and completed in July 1994; research on labour practices and CN's equipment; and the decision of "The Mediation-Arbitration Commission appointed by the Minister of Labour pursuant to the Maintenance of Railway Operations Act," dated June 1995.

For historical background, Paterson referred me to *History of the Canadian National Railways* by G. R. Stevens (Macmillan, 1973); *The People's Railway: A History of Canadian National* by Donald MacKay (Douglas & McIntyre, 1992); *Train Country* by Donald MacKay and Lorne Perry (Douglas & McIntyre, 1994); "Canadian National Railways and Via Rail" by Garth Stevenson, which appeared in *Privatization, Public Policy and Public Corporations in Canada* (Institute for Research on Public Policy, 1988); and CN Annual Reports from 1961 to 1965. I am most grateful to Carol Paterson.

Other books that proved valuable were *Liberation Management: Necessary Disorganization for the Nanosecond Nineties* by Thomas J.

Peters (A. A. Knopf, 1992) and especially *Double Vision: The Inside Story of the Liberals in Power* by Edward Greenspon and Anthony Wilson-Smith (Doubleday Canada, 1996).

Wes Kelley, CN's vice-president, public affairs and advertising, gave me the "management presentation" on privatization that James A. Runde of Morgan Stanley & Co. delivered to CN's top executives on February 22, 1995; the entire script of CN's international road show; and internal memos on the charge towards privatization. Kelley's staff provided me with excellent company periodicals that explained the reasoning behind the privatization, and its progress, to employees and pensioners.

I owe thanks to Renee-Lise Trudel, CN's director of production services. After I completed the manuscript, she did an exceptional job rounding up photographs and dealing with staff at Douglas & McIntyre. Indeed, I hereby thank the entire staff of CN's public affairs and advertising division, not only for research assistance, but for being unfailingly cheerful under considerable pressure. These people were a pleasure to be around.

I am grateful to David Todd, CN's vice-president, government affairs, for helping open ministerial doors for me in Ottawa, and to Sandra Wood, CN's manager, government affairs, for finding ministerial photos and sharing her witty perspective on certain aspects of the story. From Michael Sabia, I received the internal document "Canadian National: A Turnaround Story" (September 1995), which graphically made the case for privatization.

Freelance transportation writer Alex Binkley, a member of the Parliamentary Press Gallery, donated a hefty box of research that included a copy of the hard-to-get and "strictly confidential" Kearney report. Entitled "Canadian National: Meeting the Challenges of the Changing Transport Marketplace," the report was the work of consultants A. T. Kearney Inc., the Brackenridge Group of transportation consultants, and Decima Research.

Binkley's box also contained a fascinating document by E. G. Abbot, executive secretary of the Canadian Railway Labour Association. Its title—"CP Rail, CN Rail, VIA Rail; Management Incompetence, Government Intransigence; Railway Labour Relations, 1960–1995; Privatization Canadian National, 1995"—reads like a table of contents, but the report is no less interesting for that. Another Binkley research treasure was the "Final Report on Conditions of Work in the Railway Industry," which Donald C. Fraleigh completed for Transport Canada in April 1994. Thank you, Alex.

I also owe thanks to Robert Nault, MP for Kenora-Rainy River and chairman of the parliamentary "Task Force on the Canadian National Railways System," for a copy of the task force's 1994 report; to Barry C. Scott, director of communications and public affairs at CP Rail, for the brief that CP submitted to the task force; and to Jo-Ann Hannah, national representative, pension and benefits department, Canadian Auto Workers, for CAW's submission on the privatization of CN to the federal Standing Committee on Transportation on May 31, 1995.

For granting me interviews that sometimes lasted hours, I am especially grateful to Paul Tellier and Michael Sabia, and to several other senior CN executives. The drive towards privatization in 1995 imposed an enormous workload on them, and in late 1996, a year after they had first become officers of a shareholder-driven company, many were still working twelve-hour days. Yet they made plenty of room for me in their schedules. They included Chairman David McLean; Gerald K. Davies, senior vice-president, marketing; Jack T. McBain, senior vice-president, operations; James M. Foote, vice-president, investor relations (later vice-president, merchandise); Wes T. Kelley, vice-president, public affairs and advertising; Claude Mongeau, vice-president, strategic and financial planning; Jean-Pierre Ouellet, chief legal officer, corporate secretary; and David E. Todd, vice-president, government affairs. Ronan McGrath, vice-president, information technology and accounting, and Louise Piché, vice-president, quality and human resources, left CN for jobs elsewhere in 1995, and chief financial officer Yvon H. Masse retired, but all three gave me their accounts of the push towards privatization.

CN directors Purdy Crawford and Cedric E. Ritchie granted enlightening interviews, and I offer them my thanks as well. I am particularly indebted to two of the most influential members of Tellier's privatization "brain trust": Torrance Wylie, chairman of GPC Government Policy Consultants, Ottawa, and former Liberal cabinet minister Edward Lumley. They told me about the behind-the-scenes friction and clashes of personality that the media never reported.

Paul Martin and Doug Young, the cabinet ministers at the heart of the privatization effort, and MP Robert Nault took breaks from their wildly busy agendas, leaned back and recalled their crucial roles in the privatization. Thank you, gentlemen.

Bernard Leibov of Imagination Ltd. explained the production of the railway's international road show, and Winthrop P. Conrad Jr., CN's U.S. lawyer during the privatization campaign, described his contribution to the prospectus and to getting CN shares listed on the New York Stock Exchange. My thanks to you both.

Finally, the underwriters. I could not have written this book without the help of several investment bankers and rail analysts. They included Gordon Lackenbauer and Evan Siddall (who later joined Goldman, Sachs in New York) of Nesbitt Burns Inc., Toronto; David Wilson and Tony Hine (who later joined Gordon Capital Corp.) of ScotiaMcLeod Inc., Toronto; Gary Yablon of Schroder Wertheim & Co., New York; and John Downing, Mark Tercek and Craig Kloner of Goldman, Sachs & Co., New York. All these men were gracious and patient with a writer who was less than sophisticated about the intricacies of stock-market trading. The interviews added up to such a pleasant experience for me because nearly all the people I grilled remembered what Wylie called "the sprint" towards CN's privatization as one of the supreme adventures of their careers. A year after CN crossed the finish line, John Downing told me, "I'd love to do it again." That's exactly how I feel about this book.

As with every book I've written, Penny, my wife for forty-two years, proofread *The Pig That Flew*. She detected spelling mistakes, inconsistencies and repetition in the text, and other mistakes that, if left uncaught, would have profoundly embarrassed me. Once more with feeling, thank you, Penny.

Index